Asking
the Right
Questions
in Abnormal
Psychology

Asking the Right Questions in Abnormal Psychology

STUART M. KEELEY

Bowling Green State University

Prentice Hall
Englewood Cliffs, New Jersey 07632

Library of Congress Cataloging-in-Publication Data

Keeley, Stuart M., 1941–
    Asking the right questions in abnormal psychology / Stuart M.
Keeley.
        p.   cm.
    ISBN 0–13–291212–0
    1. Mental illness—Research—Evaluation.   2. Critical thinking.
I. Title.
RC337.K45   1995
616.89—dc20   94–30165
                                                            CIP

Editorial/production supervision
    and interior design: Maureen Richardson
Acquisitions editor: Heidi Freund
Cover designer: Rosemarie Paccione
Buyer: Tricia Kenny

Printed in the United States of America
10 9 8 7 6 5 4 3 2

ISBN   0-13-291212-0

Prentice-Hall International (UK) Limited, *London*
Prentice-Hall of Australia Pty. Limited, *Sydney*
Prentice-Hall Canada Inc., *Toronto*
Prentice-Hall Hispanoamericana, S.A., *Mexico*
Prentice-Hall of India Private Limited, *New Delhi*
Prentice-Hall of Japan, Inc., *Tokyo*
Simon & Schuster Asia Pte. Ltd., *Singapore*
Editora Prentice-Hall do Brasil, Ltda., *Rio de Janeiro*

Contents

Preface

To the Student:

For many years I have been convinced that the most important goal in education is helping students learn *how* to think, rather than *what* to think. To me, the surest way to attain that goal is to emphasize and encourage question asking behavior. When we know what questions to ask, we can then join in the conversations taking place around us, whether they are about politics, personal relationships, or abnormal psychology. As active questioners, we do not have to be sponges—passive absorbers of experts' knowledge. We can effectively talk back to those who try to persuade us and make up our minds about what we choose to believe. The biggest obstacle to our joining the conversation is not knowing what questions to ask.

Questioning skills are especially important in the field of abnormal psychology, which is much more than just an encyclopedic collection of facts and theories. It is a field in which knowledge claims are in dynamic flux and need to be evaluated by all of us who might be affected by such claims. This book is for those who want to do more than memorize and reproduce what they read and hear from the most recent expert they encounter; it is for those who want to learn to "ask the right questions" about abnormal psychology. Certain questioning strategies are so powerful that they can be used in many diverse situations and across many academic disciplines. Many of the ideas I have included in this book have been influenced by my previous collaboration with Neil Browne on a book that teaches students how to be critical thinkers across a wide spectrum of situations: *Asking The Right Questions: A Guide to Critical Thinking*. The book has been used in many kinds of courses, and the widespread appeal of this and similar books suggests that many professors highly value critical thinking skills and want their students to learn how to ask good questions. My perceptions of the positive impact of books on critical thinking and the desirability of emphasizing such skills in courses across many disciplines has greatly influenced my desire to write a critical thinking book for students in abnormal psychology classes.

Why a critical thinking book for abnormal psychology? My many years of teaching abnormal psychology and my experience emphasizing critical thinking skills have convinced me that a special critical thinking text is needed for this course. First, the best way to truly learn to think critically about a discipline is to use the material in the discipline to practice such skills. Second, most students begin their course in abnormal psychology without prior knowledge of how to "ask the right questions" about important topics in the field, such as schizophrenia, depression, and psychotherapy. Even if they have learned some useful general questions, they find encountering a coherent set of questions applied to abnormal psychology material quite beneficial to their evaluation of such material. Consider, for example, how empowered you would feel if you had a depressed relative and could ask an expert many constructive questions about the treatment of depression. Third, the field of abnormal psychology presents an exciting and unique learning challenge. It strives to understand one of the most interesting, but complex things in our world—human behavior—and researching such behavior poses unique and complicated problems. Thus, regardless of how much prior training you have had in critical thinking, you will be able to sharpen your thinking skills by practicing asking the right questions about specific claims made in the field of abnormal psychology, such as that presented in your textbook,.

My main assumption in writing this book is that the best way to learn how to think effectively about abnormal psychology is to (1) know what questions to ask about the information you will encounter, (2) to see those questions in action within the context of abnormal psychology texts, and (3) to practice asking those questions in the context of in depth presentation of materials. I have tried to stay consistent with these assumptions in designing this book.

Also, in understanding the purpose of this book, you need to be aware of two important features of abnormal psychology. First abnormal psychology texts are usually very thick and make hundreds of knowledge claims. Most of these claims emerge from an exciting knowledge seeking process and empirical research. To understand the claims, we need to understand this process in more depth than most texts provide. Also, often claims are in conflict or have important limitations. Experts often disagree.

Thus, the purpose of this book is to provide you with a list of questioning skills that will help you actively interact with your text material and any other related material in such a way that you can personally construct the meaning of the material. That is, I want to help you interpret, rather than reproduce information. The book is also designed to help you transfer thinking skills to any material related to abnormal psychology, including talk show experts, newspaper reports, magazine stories, or journal articles.

To the Instructor:

This book is meant for those instructors who want to encourage their students to actively "think about" ideas and to ask questions of the experts. It is for those teachers who highly value autonomy and questioning in their students, and want to help the students develop such capabilities. Most of my ideas about the organization of the book have evolved from many years of experience in teaching both critical thinking and abnormal psychology. I have concluded that abnormal psychology in its present state consists of knowledge claims that emerge from relatively few basic knowledge seeking strategies, and that students can become better critical thinkers by recognizing these strategies and practicing their critical thinking skills on text examples reflecting these strategies. My belief in a set of core critical thinking questions and core knowledge seeking strategies has influenced the major features of the book.

What are those features? First, the book provides an introduction to the concept of critical thinking. It then discusses within the context of sample abnormal psychology text material a number of useful critical thinking questions that students can apply to virtually any research based generalization. The rest of the book is the application of these questions to domains of specific research strategies and abnormal psychology core content areas, such as schizophrenia, affective disorders, and anxiety disorders. Each chapter highlights a research study frequently cited in abnormal psychology texts and its research strategy, while stressing critical questions most relevant to such research. Critical evaluation of the research study is then modeled for the student. This feature gives students practice in critical questioning while providing immediate feedback and alerts them to especially important issues associated with different kinds of research strategies.

Finally, to maximize the likelihood that questioning behavior will transfer to other material, each chapter that focuses on a particular research strategy provides helpful transfer of learning hints at the end of the chapter. Instructors can facilitate the transfer process by supplementing the book with learning transfer tasks.

Asking
the Right
Questions

PART I

Introduction

◆

CHAPTER 1

The Benefits of Asking the Right Questions

Imagine the following. You are watching a television talk show, and you see an expert clinical psychologist praising a new "wonder drug" for the treatment of depression. The expert claims that "studies show that this drug cures depression for most people." Sitting on your coffee table is a copy of *Time* magazine, in which the cover story acclaims the same drug. Should you immediately call that uncle of yours who has been suffering from depression and suggest that he call his doctor and request the drug?

We often encounter situations like the above, in which we must evaluate claims made by various sources. We expect a course in abnormal psychology to help us know just what questions we should ask of such claims so that we can decide for ourselves how much we want to count on them. For example, did you think about asking the following questions about this expert's claims?

> What does this expert *mean* by "studies show," or "cures depression," or "most people"?
>
> What *support* does this expert have for her conclusion?
>
> Were *samples* used in the studies supporting her claim *biased*?

What procedures were used to assess depression? How well do those procedures work?

How confident can we be that the people were actually depressed to begin with?

How severely depressed were the people treated?

Did researchers in these studies use control groups?

Are there possible reasons for the improvement of the condition of depressed people other than their use of the drug?

What kinds of important information did the experts leave out?

Do other studies exist that refute these results, or that replicate these results?

Do other drugs provide an even better success rate?

Does psychotherapy show a better success rate?

When you take part in an abnormal psychology class, you can benefit greatly—both within the class, and in your present and future world outside the class—by developing the habit of asking critical questions. Such questions enable you to better understand and evaluate the constant barrage of information you face daily. Unfortunately, reading textbooks and articles and listening carefully to lectures from teachers in abnormal psychology classes will not be enough for you to develop such habits.

Why should you develop the habit of asking critical questions? Because asking such questions provides you with many benefits, including the following.

1. A greater sense of *clarity, understanding, and focus.* For example, by asking the right questions, we get a clearer picture of just what our textbooks are striving to communicate; because by our active questioning, we create personal meanings from the material. We develop a clear picture of how the separate parts fit into a coherent whole. For example, we can answer the question, "Why is that sentence, or paragraph important," without resorting to "because it looks important," as an answer. Instead of knowing what a textbook *says*, we come to know what it *means.* Asking critical questions clarifies meaning.

2. A sense of *autonomy and empowerment.* Experts disagree. Criti-

cal thinking is how we *evaluate* experts. Thus, as critical thinkers, you actively make your own decisions and do not have to be dependent upon the last expert you encounter. Critical thinking puts *you* in control of your choices.

3. **The sense of *satisfaction that comes from active involvement*.** Knowing what questions to ask gives you the satisfaction of being an *active participant* in the community of knowledge seekers—a member of a group involved in important conversations. When we don't question, knowledge flows in only a single direction—from communicator (usually an "expert") to receiver. It is satisfying to be active in the process of making sense out of what others are communicating. It is also satisfying to know when to say yes and when to say no to an idea and to know that you have *good reasons* for making such judgments. Actively participating in the conversations of those seeking knowledge is much more enjoyable than being a passive onlooker.

The purpose of this book is to show you how to gain these benefits and others in your abnormal psychology class by learning how to ask the right questions. Because this book emphasizes developing habits of questioning, the habits you learn will not only be valuable in your learning about abnormal psychology, but they also will be habits you can *transfer* to your encounters with many life situations, such as that depicted in our opening imagined vignette. For example, when we are finished with this learning journey, you should be able to ask the right questions of claims made by research articles, textbooks, classroom lectures and discussions, mental health professionals, talk shows, newspapers, teachers, speeches, and magazines.

◆ FROM LEARNING *WHAT* TO THINK TO LEARNING *HOW* TO THINK

The material we encounter in an abnormal psychology course is intrinsically fascinating to most of us. It addresses many interesting questions and offers answers to questions that have much relevance to our lives. As rewarding as it might be to try to absorb the interesting material—the "facts"—presented in your abnormal psychology texts and lectures, it is even more satisfying to learn *how to think* about such material.

To see why this might be the case, let's explore these two divergent ways we might approach learning in an abnormal psychology course. One way is to try to absorb as much knowledge from the experts in the field as we can by carefully underlining or highlighting the material presented in our text and taking extensive notes in lectures. Our main goal is to incorporate what the experts in the field have to say. This is the sponge model approach to learning. We can see that this approach to learning has many characteristics of a sponge. It is *passive*, rather than active. It focuses on one-way absorption, rather than two-way interchange. It requires relatively easy mental work—and quick mental rewards; we get our answers quickly and relatively painlessly. When we use this model of learning, we use textbooks much like we use encyclopedias or museums; we treat them as repositories of accumulated knowledge. If we use this approach well, we often get the sense that we *know* a lot. But do we? Not really. A more precise answer is that we have lots of *information*. The key issue is the meaning of the word "know."

We do not truly know most important things until we have actively thought things through. It is only after we have learned to organize, analyze, and evaluate materials that we come to "know" that material. Thus, much of what we "know" is constructed by us as we actively think about information. We become educated by seeking and questioning, actively making meaning, rather than by reproducing other's information. Thus, knowing how to think is a prerequisite to gaining *deep knowledge*, as contrasted to *superficial knowledge*. For example, memorizing a claim by an expert that schizophrenia is inherited is not gaining knowledge. When you have assessed that claim through a variety of thinking processes and constructed the meaning of that claim for yourself, then you have knowledge. Thus, my goal in this book is to teach you *how* to think, not *what* to think!

When our learning focus is on asking questions, our learning has characteristics much different from sponge model learning. It is *active*, not passive. It is *reflective*, rather than reflexive. It is hard, often frustrating work. We have to ask many questions before we can formulate our personal conclusions. Instead of giving us quick answers, such learning often requires long delays before answers can be found. Because of the active engagement, the hard work, the long delays, and especially the value of the final product, we find it highly rewarding when we experience a sense of constructed knowledge. A major advantage of this approach is that our new knowledge is *personally constructed knowledge*; it is as though we have been given the opportunity to successfully complete a sculpturing project. This book is meant for learners who would rather be sculptors than sponges. In learning situations, one successfully constructs knowledge by asking the right questions. We, of course, will never learn to ask *all* the right questions, in the same way that we can never know all the useful ways to mold clay. We do know that over time, people invested in learning have discovered many kinds of useful questions. Thus, by "asking the right questions," I mean asking some questions about abnormal psychology that many people who have reflected on the process of critical thinking have found helpful in deciding what to believe.

If we approach learning as an active questioning process, we view claims of experts as reports of the results of an ongoing inquiry process, a process that is itself open to argument and debate. You will become an active learner in your abnormal psychology course because I will help you to better appreciate the ongoing inquiry process and show you how to ask and answer a number of critical questions about it. Throughout the book I emphasize questions that are especially relevant to inquiry in abnormal psychology.

◆ EXPERTS DISAGREE!

Not only does learning how to think make it possible for us to gain deep knowledge, asking the right questions also protects us from being too easily influenced by the last expert we meet. Remember: experts disagree! Experts cannot present us with *certain knowledge*, or with indisputable facts. They can only present *fallible knowledge claims*. We can best view such claims as ideas someone wants us to believe, which are the outcomes of imperfect arguments in an ongoing debate. And we can legitimately say to such claims, "That's debatable!" Knowing how to ask critical questions provides us with a ticket to the ongoing debate.

For the most part, textbooks choose to focus on the end results of these ongoing debates—the main findings and conclusions—and tend to de-emphasize the full inquiry process used. Thus, textbook authors are much like gardeners who present us with their choice of the best cut flowers from a gigantic garden without permitting us to share in the gardening work that goes into growing the flowers or exposing us to the wide variety of other flowers that could have been cut. Because of this, we need to question the textbook authors about their knowledge claims (the cut flowers) before we can fully appreciate their beauty, or lack of such.

In summary, we can get the most out of our abnormal psychology course if we talk back to the experts by asking the right questions. Instead of being a passive spectator of knowledge claims, we can achieve the benefits that come with being an active participant in the search for knowledge. Each of us can experience the thrill of searching for our own knowledge in the form of warranted, or justified knowledge claims.

◆ PLAN OF THE BOOK

Let me now tell you how I have set up our learning journey through subsequent sections of the book. The next chapter provides you with a definition of critical thinking that we can use throughout the rest of the book. The definition reflects much recent thought about the process of critical thinking and emphasizes "asking the right questions." When you finish the chapter, you should have a good sense of what it means to critically evaluate. Then, the next section of the book, Part II, provides you with a list of critical thinking questions that are useful in virtually any encounter with material related to abnormal psychology and elaborates on their meaning. When you have finished this part of the book, you should have a good sense of what questions you need to ask as a critical thinker and how you can go about answering them.

The purpose of Part III is to provide you with an opportunity to practice asking critical-thinking questions. Each chapter in Part III highlights a common research approach to questions about abnormal behavior as it has been applied to a major topic area of abnormal psychology. The research approaches addressed in these chapters emphasize empirical research and the search for general laws about human behavior because that is what individuals in the field of abnormal psychology are presently stressing. Chapters begin with a hypothetical passage that might appear in a typical abnormal psychology text, which is presented in the brief form in which you will usually encounter such excerpts. Following the excerpt is a discussion of the rationale of the research approach illustrated by the passage and the critical questions that are especially relevant to it. Following this discussion, the chapter presents a preliminary critical evaluation of the passage—the evaluation that is possible without knowing more about the details of the actual research. Then I provide you with a fairly detailed account of the actual research that formed the basis of the reasoning in the opening passage. The purpose of this elaboration is to give you a good sense of the complex research process that leads up to the conclusions that textbook writers infer from the research. My hope is that when you encounter other research of analogous form, you can then better appreciate what had to go on behind the scenes to produce the final research product— the findings and conclusions—and thus be better able to critically evaluate subsequent research. A major assumption that I am making is that most of the reasoning in abnormal psychology is dominated by reliance on relatively few research approaches, and you can best critically evaluate such research if you have been exposed in some detail to them.

After the detailed description of the research study, an advanced critical evaluation emphasizes the question, "How good is the evidence?" This section models the application of critical-thinking questions to the research. You will learn best from this section by first trying to answer the critical questions without reading my responses. My responses will illustrate for you the process of questioning, but will not be the *only* responses possible to each of the questions.

One of the biggest difficulties we have in learning is transferring what we learn to situations that are different from those in which we originally did the learning. Sometimes, we simply don't know how to "turn the switch" to the right set of questions, even though we have those questions at our disposal. Thus, the next section in each chapter is devoted to providing you clues for turning on the "transfer switch"—to help you recognize a match between what you have learned and the new learning situation. Finally, to further promote learning transfer, the chapter ends with another passage quite different in content to the opening passage but analogous in its research approach. You should determine how this passage is like the opening passage and then consider the questions you would pose regarding the research.

CHAPTER 2

◆ ▬▬▬▬▬▬▬▬▬▬▬▬▬▬▬▬▬▬▬▬▬

What Is Critical Thinking?

Although many of your teachers want you to be critical thinkers, they probably do not agree on any precise meaning of critical thinking. However, most of us who have given a lot of thought to defining critical thinking agree that "being a critical thinker" requires (1) *an awareness of useful questions* to ask when presented with new information, (2) the *skills* to answer the questions, and (3) a set of *attitudes* and *dispositions* that encourage us to *want* to ask useful questions and to ask them in a *fair-minded* way. I focus primarily on helping you learn how to ask questions throughout our book; however, we need to keep in mind throughout our learning journey that we are only truly critical thinkers when we also possess certain attitudes.

As we begin our journey, remember that the list of questions and attitudes that I will emphasize is a "starter" list and that such lists differ. That is because critical thinking is not a "thing" or an "essence" that exists independently of the values, beliefs, and assumptions of those of us defining it. Also, many different lists can be useful, and we expand our critical thinking abilities by remaining open to multiple lists. I therefore want you to perceive the lists as a temporary instruction kit. Such critical thinking kits have many features in common, and the kit I want to share with you overlaps greatly with most kits you might encounter. If we can incorporate this kit into our approach to learning, we will have made major strides toward becoming more effective critical thinkers.

Following is my list of critical thinking questions for the study of abnormal psychology. Each question serves as a checkpoint through which knowledge claims of others must successfully pass before we incorporate them as "our" claims. These questions are our tools for constructing our knowledge. Each will be discussed in more detail in the next section, and the list will serve as our basic critical thinking kit throughout our learning journey.

◆ CRITICAL THINKING QUESTIONS

1. **What is the structure of the reasoning?**
    a. What are the issue and the conclusion?
    b. Why do the issue and conclusion matter?
    c. What are the reasons?
    d. What terms or phrases are ambiguous?
    e. What perspectives underlie the reasoning?
2. **How good is the evidence?**
    a. Is there any evidence?
    b. How generalizable are the samples?
    c. How valid are the measures and the experimental manipulations?
    d. Are any statistics deceptive?
    e. Are there rival causes?
    f. What significant information is omitted?
    g. What conclusions are justified by the evidence?

I will discuss each of these questions in detail in Chapters 3 and 4.

You can't be a critical thinker without being aware of questions like these and without knowing how to get answers to them. However, even if we know when and how to ask these questions, we can't truly be critical thinkers until we are inclined to *want* to ask the right questions and to ask them with certain attitudes. What are some of the important dispositions and attitudes toward which we wish to strive? I have listed some of them here.

A major assumption underlying my list of dispositions and attitudes is that the purpose of critical thinking is to reach a reasoned, fair-minded judgment, rather than to tear down, destroy, defeat, or demolish someone else's reasoning. Our goal is to improve our understanding—to move forward in our conversation with those in the field. Critical thinking should enrich, not spoil.

1. *Wanting to question and being curious.* Knowing what questions to ask can't help us if we do not motivate ourselves to ask such questions, and many forces operate against such self-motivation. As critical thinkers, we must overcome these. Some major obstacles to becoming habitual questioners include: laziness, susceptibility to accepting the word of authorities, a need for harmony with and approval from others, and comfort with our present belief systems. Asking questions is hard work, challenges experts, and sometimes annoys others. We are especially reluctant to question when we already think we agree with the point someone is trying to make. We must work hard to overcome such obstacles.

2. *Openness and honesty.* Because of our needs, values, prejudices, and biases, we approach many issues with *prior commitments* that make it hard for us to honestly question our own beliefs and truly hear views contrary to ours. In the same way that we would not want to judge the guilt of a person whom we believe is guilty on the basis of only the prosecution's presentation of evidence, we want to truly give the defense attorney's case a hearing before we make our judgment. We must strive to let the evidence speak and not our built-in biases and prejudices.

3. *Persistence and high frustration tolerance.* Asking questions and getting answers to them takes time and hard work. Critical thinkers must learn to endure short-term pain for the rewards of long-term gain.

4. *Intellectual humility and flexibility.* We need to accept the fact that often we may be wrong and/or ignorant of important information, and that's okay. Human beings are fallible. Accepting the fact that we are fallible makes it easier for us to question our own beliefs.

5. *Desiring clarity, precision, and accuracy.* Critical thinkers strive to improve the clarity, precision, and accuracy of their own think-

ing and the thinking of others, recognizing that the acceptance of sloppy, vague, inaccurate ideas prevents them from successfully "advancing the conversation" to a more satisfactory understanding.

6. *Tolerance for complexity and ambiguity.* Human behavior is very complex. Thus, answers to questions about human behavior are often complex and uncertain. Many of us are predisposed to want *simple* and *certain* answers to complex questions. We like to see things as black or white, rather than in shades of gray. Thus, we are not easily inclined to embrace complexity and ambiguity as friends on our learning journey. Consequently, there is a major discrepancy between the way things are and the way we would like them to be. My belief is that we can best confront this discrepancy by reconstructing, or reframing, our meanings of complexity and ambiguity, such that we see their presence as a symbol of the uniqueness of human behavior and as an invitation to further challenging explorations.

I encourage you to reflect deeply on these dispositions. They are important components of critical thinking.

PART II

Asking
the Right
Questions

CHAPTER 3

What Is the Structure of the Reasoning?

Many researchers have hypothesized that obsessive compulsive disorder is inherited from our relatives. In fact some recent research suggests that a high proportion of the relatives of individuals with obsessive-compulsive disorder suffer from psychological disorders. For example, McKeon and Murray (1987) compared relatives of 50 obsessive compulsive patients with those of matched control subjects who had no psychiatric disorder. They found that the first-degree relatives of the obsessive-compulsive patients had a significantly higher rate of lifetime psychiatric disorders than the relatives of the nonpsychiatric control patients. For example, the former showed markedly greater rates of depression and generalized anxiety disorder than the latter. However, the prevalence rate of obsessive-compulsive disorder in the two groups of relatives was very low and did not differ. Among the 149 relatives of the obsessive-compulsive patients and 151 relatives of the control subjects, only one case in each group was diagnosed as having an obsessive-compulsive disorder. The researchers concluded that a "neurotic tendency," not obsessive-compulsive disorder is transmitted from first degree relatives to patients.

Imagine that your task is not to *reproduce* the facts of the above passage but to develop a *deep understanding of its meaning* and to *de-*

cide on the relevance and importance of its findings. What should you do? My hope is that by the time we have finished our journey, you will *know how* to ask questions about such passages that are needed to fulfill such a task and will *want to* ask these questions. In the next three chapters, we will acquaint ourselves with sets of questions for in-depth understanding and evaluation of communications we encounter in abnormal psychology. The rest of the book will then help you to apply these questions to major issues in abnormal psychology and in the process expand the meaning of the questions and your strategies for answering them.

I have selected critical thinking questions that I believe have the potential for very broad and useful application to the field of abnormal psychology and also require us to connect what you are learning to your own lives and to other important related ideas. For example, because psychology today emphasizes the search for research findings as the path for answering most of its questions, I emphasize critical thinking questions that help us evaluate and improve our understanding of research evidence.

I believe that learning is most meaningful when we can see the personal and general relevance of what we learn and when we recognize that what we are learning is connected to other interesting ideas. Thus, I have included questions concerning relevance and connections as part of our critical thinking question list.

◆ ASKING THE RIGHT QUESTIONS: UNDERSTANDING THE STRUCTURE

Before we can evaluate *any* reasoning, we must first *understand* its *meaning*. Understanding a message's meaning is much different than simply being able to *reproduce* the message. It is an active process of *making sense*. It requires us to actively impose a meaningful *pattern* on materials. We can do so by asking a series of questions. We begin by asking questions that identify what a communication is trying to do (its purpose) and how it is trying to achieve its purpose (its basic structure). Failure to identify the purpose and structure of reasoning before proceeding with determining its value is similar to failing to identify how a home was put together before judging whether the home is well built. It can't be done successfully.

In general, the most important parts of reasoning to initially identify are the *issue* (the *question* asked), the *conclusion* (the *answer* to the question), and the *reasons* (the *support* for the conclusion—usually research evidence).

In general, those who write textbooks, articles and essays, or give speeches about abnormal psychology are trying to respond to issues or questions that those in the field of abnormal psychology have judged to be important. When writers and speakers address issues important to them, they try to provide answers to these issues. Thus, we begin our search for meaning by asking: "What are the issue and the conclusion?" Once we have become aware of the issue and conclusion, we need to care about them in order for them to have personal meaning for us. Thus, we need to ask the question: "Why do the issue and conclusion matter?" When authors provide conclusions to issues, they need to provide support for them. That support is usually in the nature of some form of research evidence, but it can be in other forms, such as examples, personal experience, analogies, or appeals to experts. We can call that support the author's *reasons*. Our next question thus becomes, "What are the reasons?"

In addition, we can't truly understand reasoning unless we are clear about what all the relevant terms mean. Thus, we need to ask, "What terms or phrases are ambiguous?" By ambiguous, I mean subject to more than one meaningful interpretation. Thus, to clearly identify the purpose and the basic visible structure of reasoning, we need to ask the following questions:

- What are the issue and conclusion?
- Why do the issue and conclusion matter?
- What are the reasons?
- What terms or phrases are ambiguous?

Answering these questions gives us a picture of the *observable* reasoning structure and a reason for caring about the issue. Other important parts of the reasoning structure are *not explicit*. One very important *implicit component* of reasoning is the author's *perspective*. It is implicit because it is behind the scenes—it is not overtly expressed. By perspective, I mean the models, metaphors, and theories that guide the questions and concepts of an inquirer. Thus, our last question for identifying the structure of the reasoning is:

• What perspectives underlie the reasoning?

The next section is a brief initial guide that will show you how to ask these questions.

◆ ASKING THE RIGHT QUESTIONS FOR UNDERSTANDING THE STRUCTURE OF THE REASONING

What are the issue and conclusion?   The issue and conclusion are so closely interconnected that we should keep in mind that the order in which we try to identify each is not very important and that often searching for one helps us find the other. Claims people make do not come out of the blue. They have an historical background, and they are usually made because people are reacting to issues that are important to them. So we need to locate those issues. How do we do so? First it helps to be aware of some common kinds of issues in the field of abnormal psychology. Let me mention four important ones that often guide research studies:

1. What is the *nature* of abnormal behavior?
2. How *frequent* is abnormal behavior?
3. What *causes* abnormal behavior?
4. What *is the best way to treat* abnormal behavior?

Questions 1 through 4 are usually treated as *empirical questions.* This means that they call for answers that can be supported by carefully attending to our experiencing of the world; that is, we can collect research evidence that *relies upon systematic observations* to help answer such questions. When we say, "that's an empirical question," we mean that we can imagine completing some kind of research observations to answer the question. For example, "What causes schizophrenia?" is an empirical question if we believe research can provide the answer to it.

Psychologists also ask some important non-empirical questions, such as the following: "*Should* we diagnose people with the DSM-IIIR?" or "How should we define mental illness?" or "Is the insanity defense *desirable?*" Because these questions ask about the way things should be or ought to be, we commonly refer to such questions as *prescriptive questions*. We want to be alert to whether questions are empirical or prescriptive because we need to evaluate the answers to them differently. Throughout this book, I stress asking the right questions about empirical issues, while not directly addressing prescriptive questions, for several reasons. First, most issues you will encounter in your abnormal psychology courses will be empirical in nature. Second, empirical research is often highly relevant to the answering of prescriptive issues, and thus your being able to critically evaluate empirical research will ultimately help you evaluate responses to prescriptive issues. Third, one book can't do everything! I want this book to be a *brief* useful guide to critical thinking. Such brevity would be impossible if I were to give adequate coverage of both kinds of issues.

Now, let's explore how to identify the issue and conclusion. Sometimes writers state the issue explicitly. For example, they may state it in a heading or subheading or right at the beginning of the text. If so, you will usually find words or phrases such as: "The important question is . . ." "What causes. . . . ?" "What researchers want to find out is . . ." "How . . . ?" "Why . . . ?" "What does the evidence tell us about . . ." Abnormal psychology texts usually state subheadings as topic words or phrases rather than as questions. Often, we can usefully translate these phrases into questions. For example, a subheading under the major chapter heading "Mood Disorders" might be "The Behavioral Perspective," and another heading under this might be: "Extinction and Aversive Social Behavior." After reading the passages, we might convert this series of headings into the question, "According to the behavioral perspective, what causes depression?"

In our passage about obsessive-compulsive disorders that begins this chapter, the issue is not explicitly stated. When authors do not state issues or questions explicitly, we must *find the conclusion* before we can be sure we know the issue. Thus, when the question is not explicitly stated, the first step in critical evaluation is to find the conclusion, because once we have discovered the conclusion, we can state the issue. So let's now see how we find the conclusion and how that helps us determine the issue.

Aids to finding the author's conclusion. To identify the conclusion, you must ask, "What is the author trying to prove? What is her point? What does she claim about the world that she wants us to believe? Of what is she trying to convince us? What ideas does she support or back up with evidence?" If you could ask the writer to complete the sentence, "The point I am trying to make is. . . ." How would the writer respond?

The answer to these questions is the conclusion. To search for a conclusion, you look for an idea or set of ideas the writer wants you to believe. Usually, she wants you to believe this conclusion on the basis of her other ideas or statements. In short, the basic reasoning structure of much communication in abnormal psychology is: *This* because of *that*. *This* refers to a *conclusion; that* refers to the *support* for the conclusion. This structure represents the process of *inference*. When we critically evaluate such communication, we judge the quality of the inference. Remember: Conclusions are *inferred*; they are derived from reasoning. Conclusions are ideas that require other ideas to support them.

Reasoning is any discourse in which an idea or a set of ideas are given as reasons for another idea. We cannot criticize someone's reasoning unless there is indeed reasoning to criticize. So let me contrast for you the difference between reasoning and non-reasoning.

Examples of reasoning:

I believe that schizophrenia is inherited because it runs in families.

Idea supported: schizophrenia is inherited

Supporting idea: it runs in families

According to recent studies, the best treatment of post-traumatic stress syndrome is re-experiencing of the stressful event.

Idea supported: best treatment of post-traumatic stress syndrome is re-experiencing of the stressful event

Supporting idea: according to recent studies

Examples of non-reasoning:

Schizophrenia is inherited.

Best treatment of post traumatic stress syndrome is re-experiencing of the stressful event.

Let's look closely at a conclusion and the inference process, using our chapter-opening passage. What is the conclusion? Did you define the ultimate conclusion as: "A neurotic tendency, not obsessive-compulsive disorder, is transmitted from first-degree relatives to patients." We know this is a conclusion for several reasons. First, the passage presents other ideas, in the form of evidence, that support this idea; the writer makes an inference. Second, the word "concluded" clues us in to the fact that a conclusion is coming.

Conclusions will frequently be preceded by words that signify that a conclusion is coming. We want to be alert to the following phrases:

Evidence shows . . .	Studies have found . . .
Findings suggest . . .	It appears that . . .
Studies show . . .	Research suggests . . .
Researchers found . . .	One explanation is . . .
In short . . .	Yet . . .
Thus . . .	Instead . . .
Therefore . . .	But . . .
Consequently . . .	Rather . . .
Hence . . .	

Location is another important clue to conclusions. Conclusions tend to occupy certain locations, usually the beginning and/or the end of sections. For example, chapter summaries often restate the conclusions of a chapter and are thus an excellent source for identifying the major conclusions (and also issues).

◆ TYPICAL KINDS OF CONCLUSIONS IN ABNORMAL PSYCHOLOGY

Because issues and conclusions are reciprocally related, we most frequently encounter *two kinds of conclusions* in abnormal psychology readings: (a) claims about the way things are—often in the form of *empirical generalizations* (generalizations from empirical evidence), (b) claims about the causes of things—*theoretical explanations*. For example, the statement, "Vietnam veterans experienced an inordinately high rate of persistent post-traumatic stress disorder, an estimated 20 to 25 percent" is a *claim about the way things are in the form of a generalization* about Vietnam veterans. If we then try to explain *why* the rate is so high, we then offer an *explanation*. Explanations are *hypotheses* about what mechanisms might account for the way things are. For example, one author attempted to explain the high rate of stress in Vietnam veterans (an empirical generalization) by stating the following hypothesis: . . . soldiers were shipped to Vietnam simply as masses of recruits rather than in organized combat groups, and, once there, they were transferred frequently. As a result, they had little chance to develop a sense of group identity, which provides psychological protection against stress.

Now, let's try to determine what kind of conclusion we have in the opening passage. First, let's state the conclusion: a "neurotic tendency, not obsessive-compulsive disorder, is transmitted from first-degree relatives to patients." The conclusion *explains* the results. It offers an hypothesis about what the results mean. Thus, it is an explanation. Now that we know the conclusion, we can identify the issue. It is useful to define issues in both a *general* and a *specific* way. In my opinion, the general issue that our opening passage was trying to address was: What causes obsessive-compulsive disorder? I believe this because the researcher seems to be looking for explanations for the disorder. I can also state the issue more specifically: Do first-degree relatives of individuals with obsessive-compulsive disorder report more psychological disorders than first-degree relatives of nonpsychiatric control patients, and if so, why? Recognizing both questions helps us understand the structure of the reasoning.

Why do the issue and conclusion matter? Now that we know the issue and conclusion, we can ask, why should we care about them? Each of us may have different reasons for caring; thus, this is a highly personal question. However, in seeking to answer this question, we might think of *implications*. For example, we can ask the following: Assuming that we get an answer to the issue, what implications might that answer have? With regard to the passage that opens the chapter, knowing how relatives may pass on disorders can provide us with useful hints about how to prevent such disorders and make us reflect on how we might pass on disorders to others. Some of us may care about such knowledge simply because we may value knowledge of causes about human behavior for its own sake. Although we all may arrive at different answers to this question, asking it connects us to the issue; we see why we should interact with it.

What are the reasons? Once we have identified the conclusion and issue so that we are confident we know what they are, our next step is to identify ideas that support the conclusion, the reasons. *Remember: Reasons + Conclusion = Reasoning.* We can ask all of the following questions about the conclusion to help us find reasons: What is your evidence? Why should I believe that? Why is that true? Where is your proof? Do you have any facts to back up your point? How do you know that's right? All these questions seek to find out what ideas support, back up, or form the basis for the conclusion. Psychologists usually offer research evidence as their reasons to support conclusions because they see their role as one of seeking general laws of human behavior; and they assume that the best way to support such laws is to conduct research studies. Thus, abnormal psychology textbooks are full of examples of research evidence being used as reasons to support conclusions.

Textbooks also use other kinds of evidence as reasons, especially case study examples, appeals to authorities and experts, and personal experience. For example, a frequent method of appealing to authority in abnormal psychology texts appeals to the personal experience of practicing clinicians as support for a point. Because scientific research studies are the most frequent kinds of evidence you will encounter in an abnormal psychology course, we will stress such evidence throughout this book. However, we will also address other kinds of evidence, though less extensively.

◆ SEARCHING FOR EVIDENCE

When our identified conclusion is an empirical generalization, the most common kind of evidence we will encounter is a report of the specific research results supporting the generalization. Such reports will tell us what subjects did or how subjects performed in the study and will usually stress numbers or statistics. When our identified conclusion is an explanation, the evidence to support that explanation may either be specific research results or empirical generalizations based on specific research results.

Let's locate the reasons from the opening passage of our chapter. Because we know the conclusion, we can ask, "What ideas does the author use to make us think her conclusion is credible?" Two sets of research results work jointly to directly support the conclusion. We can summarize the structure of the reasoning as follows:

> CONCLUSION: A neurotic tendency is transmitted from first-degree relatives to patients.
>
> SUPPORTING EVIDENCE FOR THE CONCLUSION *(1a):* The first-degree relatives of the obsessive-compulsive patients had a significantly higher rate of lifetime psychiatric disorders than the relatives of the non-psychiatric control patients.
>
> SUPPORTING EVIDENCE FOR *(1a):* The former showed markedly greater rates of depression and generalized anxiety disorder than the latter and, *(1b)* the two groups of relatives did not differ in prevalence of obsessive-compulsive disorder.
>
> SUPPORTING EVIDENCE FOR *(1b):* Among the 149 relatives of the obsessive-compulsive patients and the 151 relatives of the controls, only one case in each group was diagnosed as obsessive-compulsive.

I want to note here that we do not have a *deep understanding* of empirical evidence unless *we can appreciate the methods used* to arrive at the results. Usually, however, abnormal psychology textbooks, primarily because of length considerations, provide insufficient information for us to comprehend the method. Because of this, it is very difficult for you to get a full appreciation of the complex research process that researchers must go through for their research to yield ultimate results—the "cut flowers" presented to you in your text. Thus, a major purpose of *Asking the Right Questions in Abnormal Psychology* is to provide you with reasoning samples with enough detail for a more in-depth experience with the actual inquiry methods used by psychologists to reach their conclusions, so that you can better appreciate the depth of understanding which is possible.

Knowing how the reasoning is connected—the issue, conclusion, and reasons—gives us a major start in understanding the reasoning. To understand the reasoning fully, we must ask our next question.

What words or phrases are ambiguous in this context? Words or phrases are *ambiguous* to us if we are uncertain about their meaning in the context in which they are embedded. We cannot evaluate reasoning until we have a clear grasp of its meaning. Authors often fail to clearly define their terms. Because authors often use terms that have uncertain meanings, we must always ask this critical question before we can know that we understand what the reasoning is really saying.

◆ LOCATING KEY TERMS AND PHRASES

The first step in determining which terms or phrases are *important and ambiguous* is to check for *key terms* in all three major parts of the reasoning: the issue, the conclusion, and the reasons. Another useful guide for searching for key ambiguous terms and phrases is to remember: The more abstract a word or phrase, the more likely it is to be susceptible to multiple interpretations and thus unclear.

How do we decide whether the meaning of key phrases and terms is sufficiently clear? We need to self-test! One test we can apply is the imagery test. Can we form a visual image of an example that illustrates the term? For example, in a research study, can we picture the measurement procedures the researcher is using to assess key variables? If we can't form such an image, we don't truly understand the term's use in that context. If we can form multiple, distinctly different images, then the term or phrase is also unclear. For example, researchers often report that some percentage of patients *improved* as a result of a treatment, without spelling out their meaning of improvement. Yet, we can picture many different meanings for improvement. It could range anywhere from a total "cure" to insignificant changes. It could range from measures on a self-report test to an observer's ratings of the client's behavior. Do you see how terms such as "depressed," "abnormal," and "cognitive therapy" might be ambiguous? How about the meaning of the term "obsessive compulsive disorder" and the phrase "greater rates" in our chapter opening passage?

In general, the more specifically the author spells out the meaning of terms and phrases, the better we will understand the meaning of the reasoning. Once we have a good sense of the visible structure of the reasoning, we can get a deeper sense of the meaning of the reasoning by recognizing the *perspective from which the reasoning arises.*

What perspectives underlie the reasoning? Imagine the following. The psychologist has completed the interview with her patient while two other psychologists have been observing. The patient, a young successful writer, has described her anxiety attacks and her suicidal thoughts, has answered many questions about her childhood experiences, her relationships with parents and others, and her current life situation. After the patient leaves, the three psychologists are discussing the interview and giving their impressions of the patient.

"This woman is clearly struggling with unconscious hostile feelings toward her mother," suggests one psychologist. "She needs psychoanalytic treatment."

"I disagree," says the second. "I'm convinced this woman's anxiety stems from some learning experiences, and her depression results from inadequate interpersonal skills. She needs behavior therapy."

"You're both wrong," argues the third. "Her anxiety arises from a biological tendency to experience rapid heartbeats under stressful conditions. She needs anti-anxiety drugs."

These three experts all interview the same woman and yet they "see" or "perceive" her problem in very different ways. These are not minor disagreements. Each expert holds fundamentally different assumptions about the nature of abnormal behavior, and each one "sees" this patient through a different set of assumptions about its causes and treatment. Also, each of the views may be helpful to the client.

How psychologists think about abnormal behavior is determined by their perspective or viewpoint; and despite hundreds of research studies, no generally accepted view has yet emerged. At present it is useful to view each perspective as a different set of lenses, each *highlighting* and *hiding* important elements of abnormal behavior, and to acknowledge that no super lens exists that permits us to decide which of these perspective lenses provides the best view. Ideas about abnormal psychology and the way in which they are presented greatly depend on the *perspectives* of those who communicate such ideas, such as textbook writers, research investigators, and teachers. For example, we learn a very different abnormal psychology from textbooks that emphasize biological causes of disorders (one perspective) than from textbooks that emphasize environmental causes (another perspective).

Because perspectives often are not made explicit, but greatly influence ideas presented to us, we need to be aware of their presence. For example, knowledge of perspective alerts us to what researchers are likely to highlight and hide, to emphasize and deemphasize, in their research. It also alerts us to potential biases in interpretation of data. When we know which lens the researcher is using, we can wonder how we might see things differently with a different lens.

Presently, abnormal psychology perspectives can be divided in many ways. One useful division is *theory-influenced perspectives*, or perspectives that reflect major theories in the field. To alert us later to these perspectives and their potential impact on research investigation, I list here some major theoretical perspectives that we will encounter in abnormal psychology and also the causes that each perspective highlights:

> Biological perspective: organic, biochemical, genetic
> Psychodynamic: childhood fixations, unconscious conflicts
> Behavioral: reinforcement; operant and classical conditioning
> Cognitive: irrational, or self-defeating, thinking patterns
> Humanistic: conditions of worth, social demands

A related useful set of conflicting perspectives of which to be aware is *causal source;* the viewing of causes as primarily biological, psychological, or sociocultural, or combinations of these. For example, some investigators now adopt biopsychosocial models of certain disorders, meaning they believe biological, psychological, and sociological factors interact to cause the disorder. Others choose to focus only on one of these three. Let's take a closer look at these different causal sources.

Those who look for *biological causes* will stress factors related to the anatomy, physiology, and brain chemistry of individuals, such as the following:

- genetic endowment—e. g., chromosomal anomalies
- constitutional liabilities—e. g., physical handicaps
- brain dysfunctions—e. g., biochemical imbalances
- physical deprivation or disruption—e. g., sleep deficiency

Those who favor *psychological causes* will look within the individual for hypothetical psychological structures, such as the following:

- enduring traits and needs—e. g., low self-esteem, need for approval
- motives—e. g., unconscious conflicts; self-actualizing tendency
- ways of thinking about the world—e. g., irrational thoughts

Those who emphasize *social and cultural factors* will look at how factors outside the individual have affected him, such as the following:

- early childhood deprivations or trauma
- inadequate parenting
- dysfunctional family structures
- societal reinforcement patterns
- socioeconomic status
- stereotyping

We have now covered our first set of questions. Once we have answered these questions, we have reached a deep understanding of the *reasoning structure* and reasons for caring about it. Let me list the questions one more time:

What is the structure of the reasoning?

- What are the issue and the conclusion?
- Why do the issue and conclusion matter?
- What are the reasons?
- What terms or phrases are ambiguous?
- What perspectives underlie the reasoning?

A final step in providing a deep meaning of reasoning structure is to test your understanding by paraphrasing the conclusion and the reasons. *Put them into your own words.* If you can do this, then you can feel more confident that you know what the author means, not just what the author says.

CHAPTER 4

How Good Is the Evidence?

In Chapter 3, we learned how to ask the very important general question, What is the structure of the reasoning? Once we have answered that question, we can move on to our next major question, How good is the evidence? Because this question builds on the questioning in Chapter 3, as we learn how to ask this critical thinking question, we will continue to refer back to our passage about obsessive compulsive disorders at the beginning of Chapter 3.

What most separates noncritical thinking from critical thinking is its emphasis on *evaluation—making informed judgments about claims.* We can't evaluate reasoning until we know its structure; and determining the structure was the focus of our first set of questions. Once we know the structure, we are ready to evaluate. The evaluation process requires that we learn a further set of questions.

Because reasoning in abnormal psychology relies so heavily on research studies as the source of evidence, we begin the evaluation process by asking the general question, "How good is the evidence?" We need to ask this question because the quality of evidence varies greatly and because evidence does not speak for itself. It always has to be interpreted by someone, and interpretations are subject to human biases. Our ultimate goal in asking this question is to *decide for ourselves* just what conclusions the available evidence merits.

It is very difficult, if not impossible, to establish the absolute truth or falsity of any conclusion, and many "truths" change over time. Thus, instead of asking whether conclusions are true, we should ask how well they are supported by the present available evidence. That is, we should ask, how much can we presently count on such claims? The greater the quality and quantity of evidence supporting a claim, the more we can depend on it, and the more we can call the claim a "fact." There is insufficient evidence to either strongly support or to refute many claims. In such cases, we need to make judgments about where the *preponderance of evidence* lies as we decide on the dependability of the belief.

◆ THE NEED TO EVALUATE RESEARCH EVIDENCE

When communicators appeal to research as a source of evidence, we need to remember the following:

1. Research *varies greatly in quality;* we should rely more on some research studies than others. Because the research process is so complex and subject to so many external influences, even those well-trained in research practice sometimes conduct flawed research; and being published in a scientific journal does not guarantee that a research study is not flawed in some ways.

2. Research findings often *contradict* one another. Thus, single research studies presented out of the context of the family of research studies investigating the question often provide misleading conclusions. For example, a front page headline in the *New York Times* announced in 1987 that researchers had identified the gene that causes manic-depressive disorders among a group of Amish. But this article also pointed out that "the same issue of the scientific journal (announcing the discovery of the gene) carried another study showing that the gene was not associated with manic-depressive illness in two other populations that were studied" (emphasis added). (Adapted from

Peele, *Diseasing of America.*) Research findings that most deserve our attention are those that have been repeated by more than one researcher or group of researchers.

3. Research findings *do not prove conclusions!* At best, they support conclusions. Research findings do not speak for themselves! Researchers must always interpret the meaning of their findings, and all findings can be interpreted in more than one way. When you encounter statements such as "research findings show . . . ," you should retranslate them into "researchers interpret their research findings as showing . . . ."

4. Like all of us, researchers have *expectancies, attitudes, values, and needs* that bias the questions they ask, the way they conduct their research to address the questions, and the way they interpret their research findings. Science is not a neutral, value-free, totally objective enterprise. For example, scientists often have an emotional investment in a particular hypothesis. Like all fallible human beings, they may find it difficult to objectively treat data that conflict with that hypothesis. A major strength of scientific research is that it tries to make public its procedures and results so that others can judge the merit of the research and try to replicate it. However, regardless of how objective a scientific report may seem, important subjective elements are always involved.

5. Research *"facts" change over time,* especially claims about human behavior. For example, both of the following research "facts" have been reported by major scientific sources, yet have been contradicted by recent research evidence: (a) Hostility and explosive anger heighten risk of early death from heart disease and other illnesses. (b) Peptic ulcers are caused by psychological factors, such as the frustration of the hunger for love never received in childhood. In fact, strong evidence now supports the claim that peptic ulcers are a disease caused by bacteria lodged in the stomach lining.

6. Research varies in the *degree of similarity* between what the researcher is studying in the research setting and the behavior outside the research setting to which the researcher is trying to generalize. The less the similarity, the more artificial the research, and the more difficult it is to generalize from the research study to the world outside.

As you can see, despite the many positive qualities of research evidence, we need to avoid embracing research conclusions prematurely. So what questions do we need to ask about research findings to decide whether they provide dependable conclusions? We need to ask questions related to the context of the research and to the actual conducting of the research. Let's first look at questions concerning the context.

◆ QUESTIONS RELATED TO THE CONTEXT OF THE EVIDENCE

What is the quality of the research source? Some sources tend to be more dependable than others. Usually, the most dependable reports are those that are published in peer-review journals, those in which a study is not accepted until it has been reviewed by a series of relevant experts. Usually—but not always—the more reputable the source, the better designed the study. Most abnormal psychology texts rely only on reputable, peer-review journals and on chapters in books that summarize research in such journals. Thus, for your abnormal psychology textbook, the answer to the question, "What is the quality of the research source?" will *usually* be: the quality of the source is good. However, in many other contexts, such as talk shows, newspapers, and popular magazines, source quality varies greatly and you will find this question very helpful.

How do the research findings fit into the broader network of findings addressing the research question? Research findings in your abnormal psychology textbooks have been selected within a much broader research context. Knowing that context helps us put the research into proper perspective. To put the research into a larger meaning pattern, we need to ask questions such as the following. Have research findings supporting the same conclusion been *replicated or repeated* by other researchers? Has more than one study found the same results? Findings, even when "statistically significant," often vary from study to study. Thus, we should be wary of unreplicated findings. How do the research findings fit in with other research the author presents? Have relevant studies either confirming or disconfirming the research findings been omitted? We need to know how selective the author has been in choosing studies to address the research question. Research occurs in the context of much other related research, sometimes hundreds of studies; thus, textbook authors are always being selective when they choose studies. Consequently, it would be helpful to our interpretation of research findings to know on what basis the textbook author has selected research studies. If the author does not tell us, we should examine the patterns of research presented to seek clues that will help us answer the question. For example, does the author rely heavily on certain journals? Also, does the author present single studies to prove points, or groups of studies?

◆ QUESTIONS ABOUT THE SPECIFIC RESEARCH EVIDENCE

We want to ask the following questions of any specific research study used by your textbook author to support a conclusion:

1. **How generalizable are the samples?**
2. **How valid are the measures and the experimental manipulations?**
3. **Are any statistics deceptive?**
4. **Are there rival causes?**
5. **What significant information is omitted?**
6. **What conclusions are justified by the evidence?**

I want to briefly describe each of these questions for you at this point, but you will become much more familiar with their meaning through our practice of critical thinking in Part III.

How generalizable are the samples? The generalizability of research findings depends upon the number, breadth, and randomness of events or people the researchers study. Often, researchers or others using researchers' findings *overgeneralize*. That is, they state conclusions that apply to a much broader population of events or people than the research study justifies. For example, recently some researchers examined the effect of the drug Prozac on people who were suffering from severe depression and found positive results. A subsequent claim that Prozac helps depression overgeneralizes because depressions differ markedly in severity, and the drug may in fact not be as helpful for those suffering from milder depression than for those whom were studied in the research.

The process of selecting events or persons to study is called *sampling*. Because researchers can never study all events or people about which they want to generalize, they must choose some way to sample; and some ways permit broader generalizations than others. We need to ask the following questions in deciding how broadly we can generalize from the sample.

1. How *large* is the sample? Usually, the more events or people researchers study, the more confidence we can have in generalizing to broader groups.

2. How *broad*, or *diverse*, is the sample? The more breadth a sample possesses, the more broadly we can generalize. For example, people whom we label as schizophrenic may respond differently depending on their age, sex, social class, symptoms, duration of disorder, and severity of the disorder. Thus, if researchers want to infer conclusions about schizophrenics *in general*, they should sample schizophrenics that differ in age, sex, social class, symptoms, duration of disorder, and severity of the disorder.

3. How *random* is the sample? When researchers randomly sample, they try to make sure that all events about which they want to generalize have an equal chance of getting *sampled*; they do this to avoid getting a biased sample. When events are not randomly sampled, many kinds of selective biases operate to affect who participates in the research, and these selective biases affect the outcome. Do you see how each of the following samples has biased characteristics?

   a. People who *volunteer* to take psychological tests, or to participate in a treatment program (versus those who do not volunteer).

   b. People who have been hospitalized for a mental disorder (versus those who have not).

   c. Introductory psychology students (versus the rest of the population).

An important rule to remember is: *We can only generalize to a group of events that have been well represented in the group we have studied.*

Thus, if we have studied moderately depressed women who have volunteered to take part in a study because they have read an ad in the paper, we can only generalize to this type of individual—not to all depressed persons. We need to be alert to the possibility of researchers and writers overgeneralizing. Is there any evidence of overgeneralizing in our opening passage to Chapter 3? We can't tell, because of a lack of information about how the sample was selected and how diverse it was. A strength of the sampling is its large sample size, but we should be wary of the possibility of overgeneralization in this passage.

How valid are the measures and the experimental manipulations?

Most research in abnormal psychology requires categorizing people and assessing, or measuring, them on characteristics in which the researcher is interested; thus we need to know whether our assessments in the research study measure what it is that we hope to measure.

For example, let's imagine a researcher who is interested in studying the relationship between whether someone has a panic disorder and whether someone has the disposition to relate to others in a dependent manner. To study this, the researcher needs to assess the presence of panic disorder and the presence of a dependent disposition. Thus, he gives a personality test to a large number of people who have been diagnosed by a psychiatrist as having a panic disorder and to a large number who have not been so diagnosed, and then finds a relationship between the presence of panic disorders and the presence of dependent personality dispositions. However, to be able to make the claim that people with panic disorders in the *non-research world in general* tend to relate to others in a dependent fashion in the *non-research world in general*, we must have confidence that our research measures of panic disorder and dependency match well how panic disorder and dependency are manifested in the non-research world. When measures seem to generalize to the non-research world in this way, we have traditionally called them *valid measures*. Because valid categorization and measurement is difficult to attain, we need to examine research closely to determine whether there is any reason to doubt the generalizability of the research measures to the non-research world.

Thus, in our passage in the last chapter about obsessive-compulsive disorder, we would first want to know how the researchers measured characteristics that they were interested in studying, such as the presence and absence of obsessive-compulsive disorders, lifetime psychiatric disorders, depression, and generalized anxiety. Then, we would want to determine how well these measures, as administered in the study, captured our ideas of how these characteristics are evidenced in the non-research world. For example, we would wonder whether people who score high on dependency on the personality test that was used would actually exhibit dependent dispositions in the non-research world.

In addition to the validity of measurement, we also need to be concerned about the *validity of experimental manipulations.* This concern is relevant only to research in which investigators have experimentally manipulated some variable. The most common situations in abnormal psychology in which this issue is important are studies of the effectiveness of treatments, such as psychotherapy or drugs, and laboratory studies. What we need to know is whether the experimental manipulation as carried out in the experiment is representative of the phenomenon as it exists in the world outside the research setting. For example, if a researcher manipulates the kinds of psychotherapy people get in the experimental setting, we need to ask whether the therapies as practiced in the research are like therapies as they are usually practiced outside the research setting. This critical-thinking question is not relevant to our opening passage, because the reasoning does not rely on any research involving experimental manipulation of variables.

Are any statistics deceptive?   Statistics can, and often do, mislead us. We need to alert ourselves to the possibility of statistical deception. We can do this in a number of ways. One way is to try to find out as much as we can about how the statistics were obtained. We can ask: Is there any reason to believe the numbers reported are accurate? Are there any biases affecting the numbers? Secondly, we can blind ourselves to the author's statistics and ask ourselves: What statistical evidence would be helpful in proving the author's conclusion? By comparing the needed statistics to the statistics given, we can spot statistical errors and omissions of important information.

Because it is often difficult to know just what statistical evidence should be provided, we can try something else. We can examine the author's statistics very closely while blinding ourselves to the conclusion; then we can ask ourselves: What is the appropriate conclusion to be drawn from those statistics? Then, we can compare our conclusion with the author's. A fourth helpful strategy is to compare the way the statistics are used with common kinds of deceptive statistics. Let me mention a few; you will get acquainted with more later as we evaluate different research strategies.

One is *misleading percentages*. Percentages often mislead when they fail to take into account the *absolute numbers* on which the percentages are based, or the absolute amount referred to by the percentages. For example, a 50 percent cure rate based on studying four patients possesses a very different meaning than a 50 percent cure rate based on studying 40 patients. Another error is the *misleading use of absolute large or small numbers*. For example, we need to ask whether the numbers would mean something different if they were reported as percentages or as relative to other numbers. Suppose for example, that we read that a recent survey shows that 250 psychiatrists support the insanity defense. To make sense of this data, we would need to know how many psychiatrists were sent questionnaires and how many responded, so that we could detemine what *percentage of those who responded* supported the insanity defense. A further error is *misuse of central tendency indexes*. Means, medians, and modes give us different pictures of "averages," or of central tendency. When we see references to indexes of central tendency, we should ask ourselves which index makes the most sense. For example, we would want to be quite suspicious of a mean score that was unduly influenced by several extremely high scores, relative to most of the scores. Lack of knowledge of the *range and distribution* of numbers may also lead to the deceptive use of statistics. We need to ask, "Could we make better sense of these data if we knew the range and how the numbers were distributed throughout the range?"

Another common error is to treat *differences in means* between groups as denoting the *presence versus absence* of some characteristic. For example, people with schizophrenic disorders may make more logical errors *on the average* on a test than do people without schizophrenic disorders. That does not mean that schizophrenics are not logical, and non-schizophrenics are logical. For example, neither group may make very many errors, even though the schizophrenic group makes more errors. Similarly, average differences in assertiveness scores between men and women do not prove that men are assertive and women are not assertive.

A final common important deception is to *confuse statistical sig-*

nificance with magnitude of relationship. Significant research effects and relationships vary markedly in size. The larger the effect size, the more meaningful the findings. For example, one group may perform significantly better than another group, but the performance of both groups may overlap greatly, such that many people in the poorer performing group outperform many in the better performing group. Such findings are less impressive than findings in which there is little overlap between performances by two groups. The smaller an effect or relationship, the less able we are to predict any individual's performance in the study. We can often detect the deceptive use of statistics by asking, "What is the magnitude of the effect?" Findings become more clinically significant as we become more confident that we can apply the data from the study to practical clinical situations. I have just mentioned a few ways that statistics can lie. As critical thinkers, we need to avoid being deceived by statistics.

Are there rival causes?   When we are evaluating *explanations* of research findings, the most powerful critical thinking question we can ask is, "Are there rival causes?" For several reasons, we need to ask this question whenever someone tries to explain something of interest by suggesting a possible *cause.* First, no study is so perfect that the facts can be explained in only one way; experts and nonexperts alike can examine the same facts and suggest different causes to explain them. Facts do not prove explanations; they only support them. Second, most investigators provide us with only their favored causes—ones that are subject to many biases. Thus, if we do not want to be unduly influenced by such biases, we must generate other possible causes. When we encounter any hypothesis used to explain some facts, we want to ask, "What other causes might explain the facts?"

Researchers try to design their studies in such a way that they limit the number of causes that can explain their results. However, much research fails to rule out important rival causes. We will want to be especially alert to findings used to support a particular theory. We need to remember that data only support a theory; they do not prove it. We will become more familiar with different kinds of rival causes in later chapters as we examine different kinds of research approaches. But let me give you an example to illustrate the meaning of rival causes. Imagine that some researchers have found that depression tends to occur at a higher rate for females than for males and have suggested that this difference is caused by biological differences between males and females. There are many rival causes, however. For example, women may be more likely to outwardly express depressive symptoms because of cultural expectations. Alternatively, women may be exposed to more experiences of powerlessness in our culture, and this exposure may make them vulnerable to depression. Can you think of other rival causes?

What significant information is omitted? In deciding what sense we should make out of an author's reasoning, we must be sensitive to what we have *not* been told. Incomplete reasoning is inevitable. By necessity, textbook presentations will selectively omit much information relevant to our appreciation of the reasoning. And, as we will see, even detailed accounts of original research studies omit significant information. Because what we don't know can easily lead us to faulty conclusions, we need to ask the question, "What significant information is omitted?"

What kinds of omitted information are important enough that we should ask about them? Lots of kinds are omitted. But there are two general categories that we want to be especially alert to. First, there is information concerning the *broader context* within which the particular research study or studies are embedded. Research studies do not take place in a vacuum. They are part of a connecting network to much other research. To sensitize ourselves to the potential importance of not having this contextual information, we need to ask questions like the following:

1. How does this study fit into the broader context of studies that have been conducted and are related to this topic?
2. Is this study one of many that have addressed this problem? What have other related studies found? Are there other studies that agree or disagree with this study?
3. Are there other important theories that have been proposed as explanations which need to be considered? For example, if the study to which we are attending demonstrates a relationship between some variable and some disorder, would it be important to know what other variables have been shown to be related to that disorder?

A second important kind of omitted information is information that we need to help get a more complete picture of the particular evidence that is being used to support a conclusion. One way to seek out such information is to ask questions that are related to those questions about research studies that we have already encountered. Asking questions about reasoning structure, ambiguity, details of methodology, and the presentation and use of evidence helps us discover relevant omitted information. As a general guide, we want to ask, "What further information would we need to know in order to make an informed judgment about the author's reasoning?"

Some important types of missing information include the following:

1. Key definitions. Are there definitions we need to know? Do investigators differ on definitions for key terms?
2. Details of study procedures. For example, who were the subjects? How were they recruited? How many were there? What were subject expectations? What specific measurements were used? How were tests administered? How valid and reliable were the tests?
3. Alternative techniques for gathering or organizing the evidence. For example, would presentation of individual subject data in addition to central tendency data be helpful? Would knowledge of the *range* of values be helpful?
4. Missing or incomplete graphs, data, or statistics.
5. Long term effects of experimental treatments. For example, if a psychotherapy treatment group shows a reduced frequency of panic attacks relative to a control group two weeks after treatment, does it continue to show this superiority after six months? after one year?
6. Negative effects of an experimental treatment. For example, what kinds of side effects have resulted from a treatment program for schizophrenia?

What conclusions are justified by the evidence? The answer to this question will be dictated by what we have discovered from our critical evaluation. This question can only be answered well when we know lots about the research evidence, especially the research procedures, as well as the context within which the research occurs.

Thus this question will take on much more meaning later as we address more detailed accounts of research studies. However, one can keep in mind some important points about conclusions at this point.

1. We need to remember that rarely is any *single* research study sufficient to prove any conclusion with certainty. We want to be wary of drawing any general conclusion from only one study.

2. There is no such thing as a perfect study. There will be flaws in all research. But, even with flaws, research can contribute to our knowledge as long as we have asked the right questions about the research and have critically constructed our conclusions from it.

3. We need to consistently guard against *overgeneralizing*. A useful way to do this is to *qualify our conclusions!* For example, we can qualify conclusions by specifying the population to which we can legitimately generalize (e.g., college student volunteers, or chronic schizophrenics on medication), and specifying the contingent nature of our measures (e.g., depression, as measured by self-report tests; therapy success, as measured by the therapist's assessment of progress). Let me contrast an unqualified and qualified conclusion.

TEXTBOOK CONCLUSION: Death of the father while the child is young is associated with later depression.

QUALIFIED CONCLUSION: For predominantly female individuals, whose mean age is 38, visiting their family practitioner in Winnipeg, Canada (population, 580,000) and two other smaller cities, about 33 percent self-reporting depression, the highest level of depression, as measured by a reportedly reliable and valid measure of depression, is for those who lost their fathers between the ages of 10 to 15 and under 6. Much overlap of depression occurs among groups. For example, the range of depression scores (plus or minus one standard deviation) for father living is 2.4 to 23.2, and for father died while between the ages of 10 to 15 is 5.9 to 31.9.

4. We need to recognize that conclusions that reflect generalizations from research data will almost always be *probabilistic* in nature. They will not be true in all cases. That is, any generalization will have many exceptions, or inconsistencies; and we should try to take this into account when we try to state our personal conclusions. We need to think in terms of *tendencies*, rather than absolutes! For example, the general conclusion in a textbook, "Anti-depressive medications reduce the depression in individuals with major depressive

disorder," only means that *some (but not all!)* people with major depressive disorder are helped by such medications. When we state our conclusion, we want to remind ourselves that this generalization applies only to some percentage of depressed people; there is just a tendency.

Virtually all the relationships that have been proposed in the field of abnormal psychology have been stated in terms of probabilities. They have not been stated as universal laws that apply to everyone. Phrases such as "most," "it is highly likely that," "tend to," and so forth, communicate probabilistic thinking. When we state our own conclusions, we will also want to be appropriately probabilistic in our thinking.

The fact that most empirical generalizations are probabilistic alerts us to a common fallacy that individuals often commit in judging the merits of a conclusion—the *man who* fallacy. This fallacy occurs because often we forget the fact that exceptions to a generalization do not disconfirm the generalization. Exceptions are to be expected. So, when we find the *man who* behaves differently from the generalization (e.g., the man who didn't benefit from the antidepressant), we should not be surprised and should not reject the generalization. Remember: the chain smoker who does not die from lung cancer does not disconfirm the generalization that smoking tends to lead to lung cancer.

5. A further idea we should keep in mind when determining our own conclusions is to remember that the more plausible the rival causes we can come up with, the more tentatively we should view the cause proposed by the author's reasoning. We also need to be careful how we think about causation. Most causes of abnormal behavior are neither *necessary nor sufficient* for particular behaviors in general to occur! They are simply factors whose presence *increases the likelihood of the behavior*. Thus, their presence may or may not contribute to any particular individual's behavior, but groups of people possessing that characteristic will be more likely to develop the behavior than groups of people not possessing the characteristic. For example, early parental loss seems to increase the likelihood that individuals will experience a major depression. However, many people who experience a major depressive disorder have not experienced early parental loss, and many individuals who suffered an early parental loss do not suffer from major depression.

A common way to think about causation in abnormal psychology today is in terms of *predisposing and precipitating causes.* This distinction can be useful to us in formulating our own conclusions. A predisposing cause is a condition that comes well before and paves the way for a possible later occurrence of disorder under certain conditions. For example, having parents who demand perfection may predispose us to experience depression later in life when we fail to meet high standards. All of the following, for example, may be predisposing causes: genes, childhood experiences, illnesses, and temperaments. A precipitating cause is a condition that occurs close in time to the disorder and seems to be the "straw that broke the camel's back," that is, the event that "triggers" the disorder. For example, a major rejection experience may trigger a depression in individuals predisposed to depression. Thinking about causes in this way reminds us that the many different patterns of causes may lead to the same disorder, and when we draw conclusions about the causes of disorders we should keep this in mind and not oversimplify matters. It is more meaningful to ask, "What are some of the possible complex patterns of causal factors that might lead to disorder X?" than to ask, "What is *the cause* of disorder X?"

◆ SUMMARIZING OUR CRITICAL QUESTIONS

We now have a working list of critical questions that we want to ask of the reasoning in our abnormal psychology textbook. The questions rely on empirical evidence as support for conclusions. By the time you have completed the rest of the book, you should know how to ask the following set of questions:

> *What is the structure of the reasoning?*
> What are the issue and the conclusion?
> Why do the issue and conclusion matter?
> What are the reasons?
> What terms or phrases are ambiguous?
> What perspectives underlie the reasoning?
> *How good is the evidence?*
> How generalizable are the samples?

How valid are the measures and the experimental manipulations?

Are any statistics deceptive?

Are there rival causes?

What significant information is omitted?

What conclusions are justified by the evidence?

PART III

Practicing Critical Thinking

CHAPTER 5

◆

The Dilemma of Missing Information

We cannot determine how well research evidence supports a conclusion unless the procedures used to get the evidence, as well as the research results, are provided in some detail. Unfortunately, textbooks in abnormal psychology often present conclusions of research with very little specific information about either research methods or research results. Following are three examples of presentations like those we might see in various abnormal psychology textbooks.

Example 1
Several studies have suggested that a genetic factor is involved in anxiety disorders. For example, in a family study of anxiety disorders, Harris and her co-workers (1983) found that first-degree relatives of individuals with agoraphobia were at greater risk for it or one of the other anxiety disorders than were the first-degree relatives of nonanxious control subjects. Noyes et al. (1986) also found that relatives of agoraphobics were at higher than usual risk for both agoraphobia and panic disorder.

Example 2
A study of 60 agoraphobics who had a history of panic attacks found

that many had other diagnosable disorders, such as depression, alcohol abuse, and other anxiety disorders (Breier et al., 1986).

Example 3
Labels of hysteria or conversion disorder are sometimes erroneously applied to people with underlying medical conditions that go unrecognized and untreated. Recent research suggests that as many as 80 percent of individuals given the diagnoses of conversion disorder have real neurological problems that may go undiagnosed.

Can we conclude from these excerpts that there is a genetic factor in anxiety disorder, that agoraphobics have other disorders, and that many cases of conversion disorder are misdiagnoses? Not without knowing much more about the context of these generalizations.

Note that the author fails to provide detailed information about research methods or results in any of these examples. When we ask the question, "How good is the evidence?" our answer is, "What evidence?" What should a critical thinker do in these situations? Unfortunately, in such situations we are at the mercy of the textbook writer. We can't do much directly with the text material, except perhaps to paraphrase the conclusion in the margin, place a giant question mark beside it, and answer the question, "What is the structure of the reasoning?" How much credibility to give the claims depends upon how much faith we have that the textbook writer has done a careful, relatively unbiased job of selecting research findings and our own sense of what is involved in conducting the research that is supporting the claim.

As you will see through later examples that provide both the textbook presentation and detailed material from primary sources for such presentations, you should be careful about relying solely on the textbook writer's interpretations and conclusions. So what should you do? Two strategies can be helpful when encountering missing information: relying on patterns of results and evaluating the primary sources. The first option is to apply a strategy of using patterns of findings for signs of credibility (when the information is available). For example, some argue that if a text reports similar conclusions from several different studies, then give the conclusions more credibility (See Example 1 above). However, we should be wary of such a decision strategy, because textbook authors often omit many studies that show contrary, or disconfirming results.

Thus, we rarely know how representative the presented research might be.

Also, several studies supporting, or converging upon a single conclusion do not *necessarily* make a conclusion more credible than if it were supported by a single study. The *quality* of the studies is what matters most. And published research varies markedly in the quality of the research methods used and of the interpretative process applied to the research evidence. For example, some researchers are much more sensitive to the possibility of rival causes than others. To judge the value of patterns of research results, we need to know the pattern of errors or biases in the studies. For example, if each experiment helps to correct errors in other experiments, or if each experiment is flawed in a different way and thus errors tend to "average out," then findings of consistent results tend to provide strong evidence for a conclusion. Unfortunately, when you read your abnormal psychology text, you will not have much access to specific information about how multiple studies used to support a single conclusion differ among themselves. However, it is helpful to your critical thinking to be alert to this issue. Your becoming aware of different kinds of research issues throughout this book should make it easier for you to decide how concerned you will want to be about specific research flaws in judging the merits of conclusions in your abnormal psychology textbook.

A second strategy that is particularly useful for overcoming the difficulty with evaluating incompletely documented conclusions in your textbook is to read and evaluate primary sources (that is, the original research report) of research studies that seem to be representative of the research summarized in various sections of the text. This is an especially appropriate strategy for a question in which you are greatly interested.

Obviously, it is unrealistic to expect anyone to read all, or even many, primary sources. An alternative strategy is to closely interact with certain core, or typical studies, with the hope that what we learn from that interaction can help us react to other studies similar in their rationale. That is the strategy I have adopted for helping you think critically about the evidence in your abnormal psychology course. Thus, a major purpose of subsequent chapters in Part III of this book will be to acquaint you with detailed accounts of some core studies in the field and to show you how they might be related to other studies about which you will read in your textbook.

In the rest of the chapters, I begin each chapter by presenting you with a textbooklike account of a conclusion which is supported by empirical research. I then invite you to join me in answering the question, "What is the structure of the reasoning?" Because of the incompleteness of detail about research methods and results, I can't invite you to ask the general question, "How good is the evidence?" until we first take a closer look at the actual research study. Thus, I next provide you with my summary of the research study used in the text's account, which includes enough detail about the study for us to complete our critical evaluation. We next ask those critical questions necessary to answer the question, "How good is the evidence?" Once we have completed this process, we should have accomplished the following:

1. a deeper understanding of the meaning of the reasoning,
2. a personal sense of how much we should be persuaded by the reasoning,
3. a sense of what we should be concerned about when we encounter reasoning using similar kinds of research evidence.

CHAPTER 6

General Issue: How Should We Classify Abnormal Behavior?

Research Approach: Reliability Studies

Topic highlighted: Classification of abnormal behavior

We now have a diagnostic system that is sufficiently reliable. The DSM-III, which was based on more specific, tighter diagnostic criteria than the DSM-II, showed quite good interrater reliability (that is, agreement among diagnosticians) in extensive field trials. Axis I and Axis V showed generally adequate interrater reliability, although Axes II and IV were generally weaker in reliability (Spitzer et al., 1979; Spitzer and Forman, 1979).

Heated debate rages about *whether* and *how* we should categorize abnormal behavior. The debate is very important because categorizing and labeling people has historically had powerful positive and negative consequences. Numerous factors push us in the direction of wanting to put people who we judge as displaying "abnormal behavior" into categories and to name the categories. First, classification has always been a necessary component of science, because science seeks general laws, and general laws are impossible without classifying. For example, if we want to claim that schizophrenic disorders respond well to some drug, there must be a category called "schizophrenic disorder." Second, classification has been important historically in the development of the field of abnormal psychology. Third, practitioners working with abnormal behavior notice patterns of behavior, thoughts and feelings that seem to go together or cluster. Fourth, the medical perspective is highly influential in abnormal psychology, and it highlights classification. For these reasons and others, psychiatrists and psychologists have worked to construct a meaningful and useful classification scheme; and in fact, most textbooks in abnormal psychology use that scheme as a basis for organizing chapters. My guess is that your textbook probably does so.

We shouldn't get too excited about classification, however, unless individuals making the diagnosis can agree with each other. Thus, a major question concerning classification that has led to much important research is, "How well do experts agree in their classification of behavior?" To answer this question, researchers have conducted reliability studies. A scheme for classifying disorders is most meaningful if it is *reliable* and *valid*. Reliability is much easier to assess than validity, and that is a major reason that researchers have extensively studied reliability, but not validity. For example, it is a lot easier to prove that experts *can agree* that people have a disorder, such as schizophrenia, (reliability issue) than to prove that they *really have* the disorder (validity issue). Thus, textbooks rely upon such studies as important evidence to support a reliance on our present classification system. Logically, this makes a lot of sense. If experts can't agree about which individuals fit into a category, then category names would tell us more about the biases of the experts than about the characteristics of the individuals who have been given the labels.

Because our present classification scheme relies so much on reliability studies to help establish its scientific credibility, and because so much research on abnormal behavior relies on an assumption of reliable diagnosis, we need to know how researchers go about doing reliability studies and how helpful such research studies are to us. Let me provide an important cautionary note: Even if we can reliably classify persons into diagnostic categories, we cannot conclude that the classifications are valid. *Agreeing* that something exists is not the same as *proving* that it does exist.

To study the reliability of a diagnosis, researchers rely on comparing the diagnoses that different experts give to the same group of people. The more they agree with each other, the greater the reliability. However, reliability estimates differ markedly, depending on how the reliability study is done; and some reliability results are much more useful than others to researchers and clinicians.

As critical thinkers, what we want to pay most attention to in a reliability study is the *generalizability of the results* to other clinicians and to other settings. We do this best by noting the experience and the theoretical training of the diagnosticians, the diversity of problems and symptoms exhibited by the sample of people being diagnosed, and the nature of the diagnostic procedures used.

For example, let's assume that one research study compares diagnoses made by highly experienced clinicians who have received *many hours of training* with the diagnostic manual, who reflect *similar theoretical training*, who are making judgments on people that *vary a great deal on the severity of their disorders* (e.g., some very disturbed, some showing no disturbance), and who *jointly interview* the people to be diagnosed (that is, they get to see exactly the same interview). Now, imagine that another reliability study compares two clinicians who have had *little experience* with the diagnostic manual, who *differ in their theoretical orientation*, who are diagnosing people who *have many symptoms in common*, and who *interview individuals independently* a week apart. We should expect the agreement to be less in the second case. Why? Because the procedures used in the second study increase the chance of the clinicians not agreeing with each other. We would want to generalize very differently in these two cases, taking the procedures into account as we do so.

Now, let's examine a reliability study as an abnormal psychology text might present it—our opening passage—and then evaluate the same study when we have it in a more complete summary form.

◆ PRELIMINARY ANALYSIS

What Is the Reasoning Structure?

What are the issue and conclusion?

GENERAL ISSUE: How reliable is psychiatric diagnosis?

SPECIFIC ISSUE: How reliably can we place people into the diagnostic categories of DSM-III?

CONCLUSION: The reliability of DSM-III is satisfactory.

Why do the issue and conclusion matter? If experts can't show very high agreement on diagnoses, then we should seriously question the value of the diagnostic process, because treatment and research strategies, and professional communication will be seriously flawed if diagnoses are not reliable. For example, if a diagnosis dictates a particular drug treatment, and drugs differ greatly in their effects, none of us would feel very comfortable if experts could not agree on our diagnosis.

What are the reasons? Field trials show DSM-III is more reliable than DSM-II; Axis I and Axis V showed generally adequate interrater reliability, but Axes II and IV were generally weaker in reliability.

What terms or phrases are ambiguous?
"Quite good interrater reliability." How good is it? Good enough to use for clinical purposes? Research purposes?
"Generally adequate interrater reliability." How adequate is that? Adequate for what purposes?
"Generally weaker in reliability." How weak is that? So weak we shouldn't use this diagnosis? Better than chance?

What perspective underlies the reasoning? Because our present classification system, DSM-III, DSM-IIIR and DSM-IV are heavily influenced by psychiatry and attempt to classify *disorders by identifying symptoms*, they reflect a biological perspective.

◆ DETAILED ACCOUNT OF RESEARCH STUDY

Now, let's apply a critical analysis of evidence to a more detailed account of the original research. Clinicians were invited to participate through notices appearing in mental health publications. All clinicians who agreed to complete the required work were accepted as participants. Clinicians were from all parts of the country and worked in both rural and urban settings. Over 80% identified their main professional activity as patient evaluation or care. Each clinician participated with another clinician in at least two reliability evaluations. The reliability interviews were initial diagnostic evaluations which were done before the beginning of the treatment. Detailed instructions were given to the clinicians to avoid possible biases. For example, clinicians were cautioned not to choose cases specifically because they presented no differential diagnostic problems and not to discuss a case before each clinician's independent completion of the diagnostic forms.

Both clinicians had access to the same material, such as case records, letters of referral, nursing notes, and family informants. Clinicians could either be present at the same evaluation interview (joint procedure), or separate evaluations could be done, as close together in time as possible (test-retest procedure). Each clinician recorded the results of his or her examination using the DSM-III multiaxial system.

A total of 274 clinicians evaluated 281 adult patients. The ethnic-racial distribution of the patients was: white (81%), Hispanic (4%), black (13%), and other (2%). The patients were evaluated in the following clinical settings: inpatient (33%), outpatient (34%), drug or alcohol service (10%), liaison service (6%), college mental health service (5%), and all other (12%). Inpatient evaluations were done in the following types of facilities: city or county psychiatric hospital (13%), state hospital (10%), private psychiatric hospital (47%), university-affiliated hospital (21%), and armed forces or VA hospital (9%). Most of the clinicians evaluated two patients each; 150 evaluations were done jointly.

Reliability is expressed using the kappa statistic. Kappa is too complicated to explain within the context of this book, but you should know that researchers use it to correct built-in biases that lead us to overestimate agreements when we simply calculate the percentage of total diagnoses made in which two clinicians agree. Unfortunately, the kappa value itself has little intuitive appeal. Kappas can range from 0 to 1.00. Researchers in this study state that a kappa above .70 indicates good agreement as to whether the patient has a disorder within that diagnostic class, and this cutoff of .70 has been used as a rule of thumb by many researchers. When the two clinicians making the diagnoses interviewed the patient jointly, so that they both had access to identical information, kappas ranged from .49 to 1.00, and 11 of 15 were .70 or higher. When the two clinicians interviewed the clients at different times, so that the information obtained was not the same, kappas ranged from .43 to 1.00, with 8 of 15 reaching at least .70. These outcomes are summarized below.[1]

The researchers concluded that for most of the categories, the reliability for both interview situations was quite good and, in general, was higher than that previously achieved using DSM-I and DSM-II. They added that as expected, reliabilities were higher when the interviews were done jointly, and the drop in reliability (from joint to test-retest) for most of the classes was relatively small. They stated that differences between reliabilities obtained under the two conditions might have been due to different questions being asked by each interviewer as well as the patient's giving different responses to the same question asked at both interviews.

	PERCENT OF PATIENTS	JOINT INTERVIEW (N=150)	SEPARATE INTERVIEWS (N=131)
Disorders of infancy, childhood, or adolescence	5.6	.66	.81
Organic mental disorder	12.9	.74	.83
Substance abuse disorders	22.0	.90	.74
Schizophrenic disorders	12.9	.82	.82
Paranoid disorders	.7	1.00	1.00
Schizoaffective disorders	4.5	.56	.53
Affective disorders	44.6	.77	.59
Psychoses not elsewhere classified	7.0	.85	.43
Anxiety disorders	10.5	.74	.43
Factitious disorders	1.4	.49	1.00
Somatoform disorders	4.2	.53	.66
Dissociative disorders	.7	1.00	1.00
Psychosexual disorders	2.1	1.00	1.00

[1]R. Spitzer, J. Forman, and J. Nee (1979) "DSM-III Field Trials: I. Initial Interrater Diagnostic Reliability," *American Journal of Psychiatry*. 136, pp. 815–817.

◆ ADVANCED EVALUATION OF REASONING

How Good Is the Evidence?

How generalizable are the samples? Ideally, to generalize to typical practicing clinicians, we would want a sample that was typical of them. This study's sample is large and broad (across settings, geographical areas), but lacks randomness. Selective characteristics that lead certain clinicians to volunteer for such studies may have biased the results. These include commitment to formal diagnostic systems, experience level, gender, and theoretical orientation. For example, clinicians who believe that knowing a patient's psychodynamic conflicts and defenses is more important than knowing the patient's diagnosis were not likely to volunteer for this study.

How valid are the measures and experimental manipulations? Are the reliability measures we get in this study what we want to use to measure reliability? Do they measure what we want them to measure? The answer depends on our interests. One possible question is whether clinicians practicing in the field, using their usual diagnostic procedures, would agree on diagnoses if they could somehow *independently diagnose* the same people. Then, we need to know how similar these diagnostic judgments are to those made in typical clinical practice. For example, if practicing clinicians usually make diagnoses using much less, or quite different, information, then the kappa values here do not generalize to clinical settings. In contrast, we might be more interested in the reliability of diagnoses made for research purposes. Then, we would want to know how well procedures used in this study match how researchers typically go about making diagnoses.

Also, we do not know to what extent clinicians in this study who were in the same settings followed the instructions to not discuss the diagnoses with each other prior to making diagnoses. If they shared reactions, then the reliability figures obtained are probably too high to generalize to other clinical settings. Because we want to know from interrater agreement studies how well a judgment made by one clinician will generalize to a judgment made by a different clinician who has independently seen the same client, the most generalizable procedures for determining interrater agreements in most cases is a test-retest procedure in which two clinicians independently see clients several days apart. Thus, the numbers we should consider as most valid are the test-retest values. Remember: *reliability studies vary greatly in their procedures, and different procedures yield different values.* All reliability studies are highly context-dependent.

Are there rival causes?   No. Causal hypotheses are not a goal of this study.

Are any statistics deceptive?   Yes. Some of the very high percentages are based on extremely small numbers of diagnoses. For example, the kappas of 1.0 for Paranoid and Dissociative Disorders is based on judgments of just two patients. Thus, these values are extremely unstable and have little meaning. Also, the kappa statistic is very difficult to intuitively interpret. What does a .70 kappa mean in terms of how often clinician's will disagree? Also, the focus of kappas is on the "class" of the disorder, not in the specific diagnosis. In Axis I, for some of the major classes, there are specific discrete diagnoses. However, the reported kappas tell us very little about how frequently clinicians agree in their diagnoses of specific disorders.

What significant information is omitted?   How did the clinicians decide which clients to diagnose? Did they choose difficult cases? Interesting cases? What was the average experience of the clinicians in working with disorders? How detailed were the interviews used? How typical are such interviews in clinical settings? How independent were the diagnostic judgments? What percentage of clinicians who initially agreed to participate in the reliability studies eventually submitted usable data? Were the study's participants more likely to be close colleagues who had similar training, experience, and orientations? If so, we would expect artificially high agreement. Were those who had more difficulty using the diagnostic system less likely to submit their results than those who were experiencing little difficulty? If so, the values may be inflated. Have these findings been replicated?

What conclusions are justified by the evidence?   Because of selective biases in the sampling and uncertainty about the generalizability of the diagnostic procedures used, we should be quite tentative in generalizing to DSM-III diagnoses in general. We should search for more recent interrater agreement studies to determine whether they are finding discrepant or supportive results. As we do further reading in abnormal psychology, we should remain somewhat wary of studies relying upon DSM-III diagnoses for categorizing people, always asking, "How reliable are such diagnoses?" One conclusion we definitely want to avoid here is that because we have some evidence for the reliability of some categories we thus have evidence for the validity of these categories. As mentioned previously, when we demonstrate reliability, we do not demonstrate validity!

Turning On the Transfer Switch

We will rarely directly encounter extensive reports of interrater agreement studies in abnormal psychology texts. But when we do, we will want to take a very close look at them. Otherwise, we will want to be alert to their importance whenever we encounter situations in which people have been assigned a diagnostic category by some societal expert, such as case-study discussions and research studies. When we encounter such classification, we should always ask, "What is the interrater diagnostic reliability?" We will find this a very useful question to ask in all subsequent exercises, because the dominant research model in the field of abnormal psychology is one that relies on the ability of experts to categorize people.

Transfer Study

Borderline personality disorder has a prevalence of almost 2 percent and is more common in women than in men (Swartz et al., 1990). High frequencies of childhood physical and sexual abuse are reported by borderline personalities (Ogata et al., 1990). Borderline personalities are very likely to have an Axis I mood disorder (Manos, Vasilopoulou and Sotorou, 1988).

CHAPTER 7

General Issue: What is the Frequency of Abnormal Behavior?

Research Approach: Epidemiological Research

Topic highlighted: Anxiety disorders

A phobia is a persistent fear reaction that is strongly out of proportion to the reality of the danger. For example, Ann had to quit her job on the 30th floor of an office building because her fear of elevators was so great she could not ride on them. Her fear was greatly out of proportion to the reality of the danger of riding on elevators. The most recent estimate of the prevalence of phobias is a rate of between 7 and 20 percent of the population with some phobic symptoms (Robins et al., 1984).

How many people experience a phobia? depression? eating disorders? Do men experience them more than women? When we ask how many people *presently* experience a disorder, our interest is the disorder's *incidence*. When we ask how many people are likely to experience the disorder over a lengthy period of time, such as a full lifetime, our interest is the disorder's *prevalence*.

Incidence and prevalence questions are examples of epidemiological research—the study of the frequency and distribution of a disorder in the population. Knowledge of rates of various diagnoses is important in planning health-care facilities and strategies and for helping understand the cause of illness. For example, depression is more prevalent in women than in men; this difference may provide

63

clues to the cause of the disorder. When we encounter incidence and prevalence estimates, we find that they vary greatly as a function of the context in which they are studied. Thus, we want to be wary of thinking in terms of *the* incidence or *the* prevalence as we ask the right questions about incidence and prevalence reports. The two most important critical questions we can ask about incidence and prevalence data are:

1. How generalizable is the sample?
2. How valid are the measures?

For example, we can expect different incidence and prevalence rates in psychiatric populations than in the general population, different rates in college students than in non-college students, and different rates in younger and older persons. We can also expect diagnostic judgments to vary as a function of clinicians' experience and training and as a function of the procedures used to determine the diagnosis. For example, diagnoses based on questionnaires may differ from those based on intensive interviews. Because they require reliance on retrospective self-reports, prevalence rates present the further generalizability problem of memory loss and distortion. An additional problem in getting incidence and prevalence rates is that we must rely on people to tell us the truth about some very personal experiences. Because of this, we can expect biases in sampling and errors in reporting. Also, making judgments about the presence or absence of a symptom is a complex, subjective process, helping create difficulties in achieving reliable and valid diagnoses.

Let's outline the structure of our opening passage, then read and evaluate a lengthier passage describing a prevalence study.

◆ PRELIMINARY EVALUATION

What is the Structure of the Reasoning?

What are the issue and conclusion?

GENERAL ISSUE: What is the prevalence of abnormal behaviors?
SPECIFIC ISSUE: What is the prevalence of phobic disorders?

CONCLUSION: The prevalence is about 7 to 20 percent for most phobias, but about 1 percent for severe phobias (empirical generalization).

Why do the issue and conclusion matter?   Answering this question has personal, scientific, and health-policy implications. Variation of such rates across temporal and situational contexts provides clues to etiology and can serve as base rates for family genetic studies. In health-care policy, such rates are useful in planning health programs and in evaluating the impact of community treatment programs.

What are the reasons?   A research study, unspecified.

What terms or phrases are ambiguous?

"Some phobic symptoms." How severe?

What perspectives underlie the reasoning?   Because the emphasis is on prevalence of disorders; the passage reflects a biological perspective.

◆ DETAILED ACCOUNT OF STUDY

Now, let's examine a more complete account of a prevalence study. Robins et al. (1984) report on the lifetime prevalence of specific psychiatric disorders in the community as found in three large household samples. They state the goal of their report as follows: (1) What is the lifetime prevalence of 15 DSM-III diagnoses in three metropolitan areas? (2) What are the major demographic correlates of these disorders? By demographics the researchers mean characteristics of human populations such as age, sex, and income. (3) What notable intersite variation exists, and how can it be explained? They define the lifetime prevalence of a particular disorder as the proportion of persons in a representative sample of the population who have ever experienced that disorder up to the date of assessment. Our focus will be on the researchers' reports of phobic disorders.

The researchers sampled households in New Haven, Connecticut (N = 3,058), St. Louis (N = 3,004), and Baltimore (N = 3,481), selecting samples from official community mental-health catchment areas, which together were to contain a population of 200,000 or more in each site. They stated that only the New Haven site was "coincident with a standard metropolitan area." Johns Hopkins University chose three contiguous catchment areas, one with a preponderance of poor blacks, one composed largely of working-class, white ethnic groups, and one with a middle-class population, all within the city limits of Baltimore. Washington University chose three noncontiguous catchment areas on the basis of their variation in degree of urbanization and social status. One area is the most disadvantaged in the state of Missouri, the inner-city area of St. Louis; the second is an inner suburb, composed of working-class and middle-class housing adjacent to the city of St. Louis, and the third is a three-county small-town and rural area on the outskirts of the St. Louis metropolitan area. Sites used varying methods of area sampling to select households and respondents within households.

Interview methods and questions were quite similar—though not identical—across settings. All sites used lay interviewers who were carefully trained over a two-week period. Interviewers used the Diagnostic Interview Schedule (DIS), used by the National Institute of Mental Health to estimate the lifetime prevalence of specific mental disorders in the general population. Its administration by lay interviewers has been found approximately equivalent in diagnostic results to its administration by psychiatrists. Interviewers ask respondents whether they have ever had each symptom that serves as a criterion for the diagnoses covered. Whenever the respondent admits to a symptom, the interviewer then asks a set of standard probes to assess whether criteria were met for possible psychiatric importance (that is, was the symptom severe enough to be of clinical interest, and did it occur at least once when it had no definitive physical cause?). The age range covered was 18 years or older in each site. The number and variety of symptoms of possible psychiatric importance experienced were compared with DSM-III criteria. Multiple diagnoses were allowed. Most diagnostic questions were identically worded, and they were presented to respondents in the same order. Similar completion rates (75% to 80%) were achieved at each site.

Researchers reported that lifetime prevalence rates for phobia were 7.8% (New Haven), 23.3% (Baltimore), and 9.4% (St. Louis) and that phobias were significantly more frequent in Baltimore than the other two areas. Rates of agoraphobia and simple phobia were significantly higher for women than men in all sites. Age, race, and urbanization (rural versus city) did not show strong correlations with prevalence of phobias.

◆ ADVANCED EVALUATION

How Good Is the Evidence?

How generalizable is the sample?   This is an ambitious study. Major efforts have been made to achieve size (in thousands), breadth, and randomness of sample, and the high completion rates reduce biasing effects. The large differences among cities suggest prevalence rates which depend upon what area of the country is sampled. This large variability suggests a need to sample more areas before generalizing about the prevalence rate of phobias. Another minor sampling bias is introduced by the omission of institutionalized individuals, who would be expected to have a higher rate of phobias.

How valid are the measures?   The research report provides no reliability or validity information about lay interviewers in general, or about these lay interviewers in particular, regarding the use of the DIS. In fact, the report gives no specific information about the lay interviewers, other than that they were carefully trained. It does state that administration of the DIS by lay interviewers has been found approximately equivalent in diagnostic results to its administration by psychiatrists. However, we do not know how much credibility to give to that report without taking a closer look at it. We also need to have some clarification of the phrase "approximately equivalent." We should have major concerns about both consistency and generalizability of self-reports about phobic symptoms based on memory, especially since researchers are asking highly personal questions that call for recall of past events. We should also wonder whether interviews by clinicians might have given us different findings than interviews by laypeople, who are not as likely to be as sensitive to interview clues about symptoms—or perhaps too sensitive.

What significant information is omitted?   How were the questions worded? Were they leading in any way? What were the age, gender, race, and social class of the interviewers? What do other prevalence studies tell us? Has the definition of phobia changed over time?

What conclusions are justified by the evidence? We can conclude that when we rely on interview reports of symptoms and study metropolitan areas in the East and in the Midwest, the lifetime prevalence of phobias can vary markedly from one area to another, ranging from 7.8 to 23.3 percent. We can't tell from this data how many of these people would see their phobic symptoms as so debilitating that they would want to seek professional help for them. We would want to see prevalence rates from other kinds of settings and from other parts of the country to get a clear sense of the range of prevalence of phobias.

Turning on the Transfer Switch

One out of four Americans will someday suffer from major depression! Over 10 percent of Americans are alcoholics!

Every chapter in your abnormal text that addresses a mental disorder will probably cite the incidence and/or prevalence of the disorder. When public figures are trying to alert us to the magnitude of some mental-health problem, they will frequently begin their talk or essay with a reference to the magnitude of the problem in terms of its frequency. Whenever we encounter such references to how many people suffer from a disorder or will suffer from a disorder in their lifetime, we want to turn on our epidemiology critical thinking switch. We want to be especially alert to terms like *prevalence,* and *incidence.* We want to keep in mind that the estimates used are greatly influenced by the diagnostic methods (e.g., questionnaires versus interview; professionals versus layperson), sampling procedures, and definitions of the disorder used. We want to be especially alert to *shifts in definition* as a possible explanation for changes in prevalence and incidence reports over time. For example, the DSM-III definition of schizophrenic disorder is quite different from the DSM-II definition, and thus incidence and prevalence data using DSM-III as the criterion can be expected to be quite different from such data using DSM-II, sampling exactly the same population.

Transfer Study
Eating disorders are on the rise in our society. Surveys indicate that 41 percent of young working women report binge eating and that between 2 and 6 percent of females in general develop a full bulimia nervosa syndrome.

CHAPTER 8

♦

General Issue: What Causes Abnormal Behavior?

Research Approach: Correlational Studies

Topic highlighted: Psychological factors and health

Many studies have found that the Type A behavior pattern places people at greater risk for Coronary Heart Disease (CHD) than the Type B behavior pattern. One of the primary studies that supported the Type A-CHD connection was the Western Collaborative Group Study. The study followed 3,200 initially healthy men for eight and one-half years. Type A behavior-pattern men in the study showed twice the incidence of CHD and five times the incidence of recurrent heart attacks throughout the period (Rosenman et al., 1975).

Recently, the media was abuzz with reports of scientists finding a *significant positive correlation* between baldness and proneness to heart attacks for middle-aged American males—the greater the level of baldness, the greater the probability of a heart attack. Did this mean that going bald *causes* our heart to go bad? Or that having a bad heart *causes* us to lose our hair? Or that something in our genes that causes baldness is related to something in our genes that causes heart problems? Or that we could reduce our risk of heart attacks by wearing wigs, or by buying a bottle of Hair-Grow? This report should remind us well of the difficulties of making sense out of research that looks for correlations between responses to one measure with responses to another measure, research that is very common in the field of abnormal psychology.

What is the logic of a correlational study? Usually, it looks something like the following. If I am on the right track with my theory that X causes Y, then it should be true that measures of X should correlate, or be associated with, measures of Y; that is, I should be able to predict Y from my knowledge of X. So, I will test my theory by getting measures of X and Y from the same people, and then I will calculate a correlation coefficient, which will provide me with an idea of how strongly X and Y correlate.

This is pretty straightforward logic. The only problem is that even though a correlation may be consistent with the researcher's theory, it also may be consistent with lots of other theories or hypotheses. That, of course, is a problem with all kinds of research, but it is a special problem with correlational research. Why? Because the researcher has not manipulated any characteristic of interest, and thus she has not ruled out, or controlled for, many rival causes. The most important caution you want to remember about correlational research is this: *Correlation between measures of characteristics does not prove causal connections between the characteristics!* Because of this, the most important critical thinking question we can ask about studies that are correlational in nature is the following.

◆ WHAT ARE THE RIVAL CAUSES?

Before you can critically evaluate a correlational study, you need to be able to recognize one. Some clues should help you. All of the following are clues to the presence of a correlational study:

- The researcher has not manipulated those characteristics for which she wants to show a relationship. This means that whatever characteristics the researcher is interested in, the subjects *bring to the research* a particular level of that characteristic; the level has not been manipulated by the researcher. For example, in our previous example of baldness, subjects were naturally either bald or not bald; the researcher could not directly manipulate or control the level of baldness.

- At least two research measures, and often many more, have been supplied by each person—either at the same time, or at two different points in time.
- The researcher uses correlational language, such as reporting results as correlation coefficients, and stresses terms like *relationships, associations,* or *predictions* in discussion of the study.

Once we have recognized that a study is correlational in nature, we need to be sensitive to the possibility of at least four different reasons why two measures might correlate. I will illustrate these four using the outcome of a recent correlational study. Researchers recently reported that smoking was correlated with suicide. The analysis showed that among nonsmokers, there were 1.09 suicides per 100,000 person years. The suicide rate increased steadily with the number of cigarettes smoked, reaching 3.78 suicides per 100,000 person years for people who smoked three packs of cigarettes a day. I will use X to refer to cigarettes smoked, and Y to refer to suicidal disposition.

1. *X might indeed be a cause of Y.* Maybe there is something in nicotine that affects the brain's biochemistry, which affects the person's mood, such that smoking (X) causes suicide (Y).

2. *Y might be a cause of X.* Maybe the more depressed and suicidal one feels, the more likely one is to smoke cigarettes, such that feeling suicidal (Y) causes smoking (X).

3. *Some other factor or factors might affect both X and Y in the same way, causing them to correlate.* Maybe one's education and social class situation affects whether and how one smokes as well as how depressed one tends to feel. Or perhaps increases in stress increase both cigarette smoking and suicidal tendencies.

4. *X and Y influence each other in some complex way.* Maybe as people start feeling more depressed, they smoke more cigarettes, and they get down on themselves for smoking, which then makes them feel worse about themselves, etc.

I suspect that it was pretty easy for you to see in the above example that correlations can be very misleading as proof about what causes what. In fact, when I tell you that a 1993 article in the journal *Lancet* reported that studies have found 280 "risk factors" for coronary heart disease alone, including low birth weight, abstinence from alcohol, and poor dental health (*The Wall Street Journal,* 7/12/93), you should be even more convinced. However, the limitations of correlational evidence are often not so obvious. When the causal link or the theoretical interpretations make good sense to us, or when we have strong pre-existing biases, it is tempting to accept correlations as evidence of causation. Now, let's critically evaluate our chapter's opening passage, remembering that correlation does not necessarily imply causation, or at least the particular causation stressed by the researcher.

◆ PRELIMINARY ANALYSIS

What is the Reasoning Structure?

What are the issue and conclusion?

> GENERAL ISSUE: What causes heart disease?
>
> SPECIFIC ISSUE: Is the Type A behavior pattern a risk factor for heart disease?
>
> CONCLUSION: The type A behavior pattern places people at greater risk for CHD than the Type B behavior pattern.

Why do the issue and conclusion matter?   Heart disease is one of the biggest causes of death in the United States. If we can identify factors that cause heart disease, then we can take steps to prevent it.

What are the reasons?   A research study followed 3,200 initially healthy men for eight and one-half years. Type A behavior-pattern men showed twice the incidence of CHD and five times the incidence of recurrent heart attacks.

What words or phrases are ambiguous?

"Initially healthy men."   We would like to know more specifics about these men, such as age, fitness, weight, etc.

What perspectives underlie the reasoning?   Multiple perspectives, but especially a psychological one, because of its emphasis on personality characteristics.

◆ ADVANCED EVALUATION

Detailed Account of Study

The Western Collaborative Group Study (WCGS) was initiated in 1960–1961 as a prospective epidemiological investigation of CHD incidence in 3,524 men, aged 39 to 59 years at intake, and employed in ten California companies. The researchers were interested in comparing how well different variables would predict the future incidence of coronary heart disease (CHD). They were especially interested in how well Type A pattern behavior, which they describe as composed primarily of competitiveness, excessive drive, and an enhanced sense of time urgency, would predict the later occurrence of CHD.

Researchers collected data during an initial meeting with a participant, called the intake, and annually until the study was completed, providing eight to nine years of follow-up. The intake studies took eighteen months, from June, 1960 to December, 1961. Researchers studied 3,154 initially well subjects whom they had judged as at risk for CHD, 2,249 of whom were aged 39 to 49, and 905 aged 50 to 59 years. The researchers determined that 257 of the subjects had suffered demonstrable CHD during the follow-up period. The remaining subjects were considered to be non-CHD cases.

Nine of the participating business organizations were in the San Francisco-Oakland Bay area and two in the Los Angeles area. The following industries were sampled: aerospace development, construction, paint manufacturing, food chain, industrial, petroleum, banking, airline, utility, and aircraft manufacturing. A letter to each employee explained the purposes of the study and invited his participation if he was free of known CHD or other serious illness. Of all those invited, 66 percent agreed to participate.

The socioeconomic and medical history of each subject was obtained, and he was scheduled for study on the organization premises by a field team, which obtained fasting blood samples and pertinent cardiovascular data. Two procedures were used to assess overt behavior pattern: a tape-recorded personal interview requiring thirty minutes and a psychophysiological test. The interview asked questions about the intensity of ambitions, competitiveness, urgency of deadlines, and hostility. For example, one interview question was: "When you are in your automobile, and there is a car in your lane going far too slowly for you, what do you do about it? Would you mutter and complain to yourself? Honk your horn? Flash your lights? Would anyone riding with you know that you were annoyed?" The interviewer asks the questions in a manner that is abrupt and fast-paced and pushes the respondent with challenging, probing, follow-up questions, delivered in a pressured fashion, and interrupts the subject now and then in the middle of an answer to keep things moving and to try to elicit hostility. The subjects' reactions to the interview are viewed as an important part of the assessment. At the end of the interview, the interviewer makes a judgment as to whether the person is Type A or B.

The final assessment of the behavior pattern was made by one of the researchers after (1) listening to the tape-recorded personal interview, (2) studying the interviewer's description and personal estimate of the subject's general behavior and motor actions during the interview, and (3) studying the independently derived assessment of the behavior pattern provided by the psychophysiological test. The behavior pattern was classified at intake and was made without knowledge of other intake history or measurement to avoid possible bias introduced by knowledge of subjects' other attributes. Personal interviews were repeated in the first follow-up study in 1962 by interviewers not having access to the initial study. The initial and repeat personal interviews were found to be similarly assessed in 80.5 percent of the subjects. Researchers assessed 1,589 people as Type A and 1,565 people as Type B.

All electrocardiograms were screened by a cardiologist, while those considered definitely or probably indicative of heart attack were referred to an independent medical referee who was solely responsible for all diagnoses of manifest CHD. This selection was made in the absence of any knowledge of the variables under investigation.

An examination of how well behavior patterns predicted CHD eight and one-half years later showed that in the younger group, Type A behavior was significantly associated with incidence of both symptomatic and unrecognized heart attack, but not with chest pain. In this group, researchers found a total of 52 Type A subjects and 27 Type B subjects with symptomatic heart attacks and 27 Type A and 14 Type B with unrecognized heart attacks. These numbers translate to 5.7, 2.7, 3.0, and 1.4, respectively, with an average annual rate per 1,000 subjects at risk. In the older group, Type A subjects had significantly more symptomatic CHD. A total of 41 Type A subjects (14.0 incidence) and 15 Type B subjects (7.3 incidence) evidenced symptomatic infarctions and 21 Type A subjects (4.7 incidence) and 5 Type B subjects (1.5 incidence) evidenced chest pain. In terms of total number of subjects with CHD, in the younger age group, there were 95 subjects (10.5 incidence) with Type A and 50 subjects (5.0 incidence) with Type B; and in the older age group, the numbers were 83 subjects (18.7 incidence) and 29 subjects (8.9 incidence.)

Because the researchers were aware that these correlations might be due to the association of Type A behavior with other risk variables, they applied statistical techniques that allowed them to determine whether the relationships indeed were due to such associations for the following variables: parental history of CHD, current cigarette usage, systolic and diastolic blood pressure, serum levels of cholesterol and triglyceride, and b-/a-lipoprotein ratios. The results of these rather complex analyses indicated that the predictive relationship of the behavior pattern to the CHD incidence could not be "explained away" by other risk factors. That is, Type A and CHD incidence were not correlated because of the influence of any of these third variables.

The researchers concluded that the pathogenetic force of Type A behavior on the CHD incidence is due primarily to factors other than the classical risk factors, perhaps operating through various neurohormonal pathways. They argue that it seems clear that behavior pattern A indicates a pathogenetic force operating in addition to, as well as in conjunction with, the classical risk factors and conclude that the findings would appear to have important clinical implications for the primary prevention of CHD.

◆ ADVANCED EVALUATION

How Good Is the Evidence?

How generalizable is the sample?   Sample size is large, but lacks breadth and randomness. (Selecting an intake age range of 39 to 59 provided a broad age range.) Most participants were from businesses in the San Francisco-Oakland Bay area of the country, restricting breadth; and all were volunteers, greatly restricting randomness. Thus, volunteer Type A's and Type B's from this restricted area may possess characteristics not typical of Type A and Type B people in general. We should ask, are there any characteristics that would lead these people to volunteer that would make them different from non-volunteers, and are there any characteristics of Northern California workers that might distinguish them from workers in other parts of the country? Might we have gotten different results from men working in other kinds of businesses?

How valid are the measures and experimental manipulations? How valid are the measures of Type A pattern in this study? The 80.5 percent agreement between different interviews from initial assessment to follow-up suggests that constructions of personality pattern determined by these assessments generalize quite well across different assessors and across time, but there is disagreement on almost 20 percent of the cases. However, as mentioned previously, interrater agreement does not imply validity. Further data showing, for example, that judgments of personality patterns from interviews and psychophysiological responses correlate with independent ratings of the same patterns based on extensive observations would better establish the validity of this measurement procedure. How much faith we place in this measure depends a great deal on how much faith we have in individuals revealing such personality patterns in a brief interview. Determination of CHD by electrocardiograms is a well-established procedure to assess the condition of the heart. There were no experimental manipulations in the study.

Are there rival causes? A strength of this study is that the researchers recognized that Type A subjects might have a tendency to have other health-risk factors to a greater extent than Type B subjects and that this might account for the behavior-pattern CHD risk. They made statistical adjustments for all the following rival causes: parental history of CHD, current cigarette usage, systolic and diastolic blood pressure, serum levels of cholesterol and triglyceride, and b-/a-lipoprotein ratios. None of these factors could account for the relationship between behavior pattern and CHD. However, some other factors were not considered. For example, they did not adjust for some associated behavior patterns, such as the way one expresses anger, amount of drug usage, and sexual behavior.

Are any statistics deceptive? Yes. Although the magnitude of the differences is quite large, we have to be quite careful in interpreting the actual risk of CHD in a Type A personality. What the findings reveal is differences in the *relative* risk; and the relative risk for both groups is very low! Even though twice as many subjects who developed CHD were rated as Type A than as Type B, the overwhelming majority of Type A individuals did *not* develop CHD; rather, Type A personality was *one* of many significant risk factors (of many) in developing CHD. If there are many other risk factors, it is very difficult to assess the relative importance of this one. Also, half as many Type B's as Type A's *do* develop CHD.

What significant information is omitted? *After* an initial coronary attack, do Type A subjects die more often from CHD than Type B subjects? (Some recent research on this same group of men has found just the opposite!) How does the magnitude of effect of the Type A/Type B behavior pattern compare to the magnitude of effect of numerous other risk factors? Are there some specific components of the heterogeneous Type A pattern that are more predictive of CHD than others?

How does this research fit into the context of other research examining Type A and Type B patterns? The importance of the omitted information question is well illustrated by research investigating Type A/Type B differences. For example, more recent, large-scale studies have failed to confirm the connection between Type A/Type B and CHD (e. g., Shekelle et al., 1985). A 1988 *New England Journal of Medicine* study reported that Type A personalities were at lower risk for recurrent heart attacks than Type B. They found that five Type B patients died for every three Type A patients!

What conclusions are justified by the evidence? We have to be very careful not to overgeneralize here. We can conclude that for men who lived in California during a particular period of time and worked in the kinds of occupations sampled here, those judged by others as having a Type A personality had a greater likelihood of CHD than those judged as having a Type B. Because the study was correlational and multiple causes could explain the outcome, we must not draw causal conclusions. We also should not draw the conclusion from this study that we can cut down our own risk of CHD by trying to change our "personality" to Type B. We also should keep in mind that most people judged as having a Type A personality are not at high risk for CHD.

Turning on the Transfer Switch

Cues to correlational studies: "The best predictors are. . . ." "Depression is asssociated with. . . ." Words like "prediction," "correlation," "association," "relation," and "link" all should alert us to the possibility of reasoning that relies on correlational research. We should turn on our critical-thinking switch when we encounter these efforts to support causal explanations.

> *Transfer Study*
> How can we predict suicide? Some people with major mood disorders commit suicide, but most do not. Researchers studied approximately 1000 people with major mood disorders to examine the factors that distinguish those who later committed suicide from those who did not. They assessed characteristics shortly following admission to treatment. The factors that emerged as significant predictors of later suicide included a sense of hopelessness, loss of pleasure or interest, fewer prior episodes of mood disorder, loss of reactivity, fewer friendships during adolescence, and presence of mood swings.

CHAPTER 9

◆━━━━━━━━━━━━━━━━━━━━━━━━━━━━━━

General Issue: What Causes Abnormal Behavior?

Research Approach: Analogue Research

Topic highlighted: Depression

Many cognitive theories, such as learned helplessness theory, assume that depressed people see situations inaccurately, and this leads them to believe they have little control over events in their world. However, some researchers have found that depressed persons are more accurate than nondepressed persons in estimating the relationship between their actions and the outcomes of situations. For example, in a series of studies by Alloy and Abramson (1979), depressed students did not underestimate the degree of control their responses exerted over outcomes. Indeed, the depressed subjects were very accurate in these judgments. Instead, it was the nondepressed students who revealed inaccuracies, believing themselves to have greater control or less control than was actually the case in different situations. Alloy and Abramson summarized their findings as follows. . . . depressed people are "sadder but wiser" than nondepressed people. Nondepressed people succumb to cognitive illusions that enable them to see both themselves and their environment with a rosy glow (pp. 479–480.)

If we were interested in whether fertilizing soil influenced growth of corn, we could do a controlled experiment directly on cornfields in such a way that we could determine the effect of the fertilizer. For example, we could randomly assign sections of large cornfields to fertilizer or non-fertilizer treatments, keeping all other conditions constant. That is, we could do things to make sure the two sets of fields *differ on the average in only one way*—presence or absence of fertilization. We could then compare corn growth in fertilized and non-fertilized fields and determine whether our fertilizer influenced growth. We would be especially impressed if all corn in all fertilized fields grew higher than all corn in all non-fertilized fields.

Now, imagine that we want to do a controlled experiment on the influence of some child-rearing practice on the development of abnormal behavior. Can we randomly assign children to two kinds of parent styles, for example, permissive versus strict? Or abusive versus non-abusive? No. It would clearly not be ethical! In fact, despite the many highly desirable qualities of scientific experiments, it is ethically and practically impossible to conduct real-life experiments to test most hypotheses about the development of abnormal behavior. However, to get *some* of the benefits of the experiment, we can apply an analogue experiment to questions of interest.

In an analogue experiment, researchers try to produce, under controlled conditions, phenomena that they believe are analogous to naturally occurring phenomena of interest. That is, they experimentally manipulate in a laboratory, or artificial setting, some variable that they believe has clinical interest (an independent variable) and determine its effect on some clinical behavior of interest (the dependent variable), trying to control the laboratory setting so that they minimize the number of rival hypotheses that explain the behavior of interest.

One of the biggest advantages to laboratory models is that they can isolate to a great extent the cause of an event, ruling out many rival hypotheses by control procedures. Their biggest weakness is that, as laboratory creations, they are not the natural phenomenon, they are only a model, or an analogy of it. Also, because researchers often use animal subjects in laboratory models, they must infer in such cases that humans and the species being investigated are similarly susceptible to the experimental manipulations.

We want to be especially conscious of asking certain kinds of questions about laboratory model research. The most important thing we want to remember is that phenomena studied in the lab are analogous to phenomena studied outside the laboratory *in only some ways;* like all analogies, the two things being compared are never identical in all ways. For example, a common kind of analogue experiment is to show that we can do things in the laboratory that lead to temporary abnormal behavior. We can, for example, induce a panic attack in the lab by having subjects hyperventilate. We then reason that if pathology can be experimentally induced by such a manipulation, the same process, existing in the natural environment, might well be a cause of the disorder. However, because the things we are comparing in any analogue study are alike in only some ways, we need to ask two major validity questions of all experimental analogue research:

1. How validly does the experimental manipulation—the independent variable—reflect some true environmental experience?
2. How validly does the clinical behavior in the laboratory—the dependent variable—reflect clinical problems outside the laboratory?

For example, if we find that certain laboratory conditions induce behaviors in animals that look like depression in human beings, we need to know how similar those conditions are to conditions human beings encounter and how similar the animal behaviors are to human behavior.

In one common type of analogue study, researchers select subjects because they believe they are similar to clinical patients with certain diagnoses. For example, much research has been conducted with college students who are selected for study because they score high on paper-and-pencil measures of clinical phenomena, such as anxiety, depression, or eating disorders. The question we must ask is whether students who self-report anxiety or depression are sufficiently similar to clinical populations with anxiety or depressive disorders for us to generalize about the latter.

In addition to questions of validity of measurement and manipulation, there are several other special concerns we should have in drawing warranted conclusions from analogue research with volunteer subjects or with convenience sample subjects, such as college students. In such research, what we often have is *random assignment* of subjects to conditions, but not *random samples* of subjects! Many important, selective, biasing factors determine such samples. For example, many studies use college students who are members of introductory psychology classes who sign up for experiments as part of their course requirements. You may have volunteered for such studies. Can you think of a number of ways these individuals may differ from a random sample of people their age? Do any of the following come to mind? suspiciousness of researchers' motives? suggestibility? seriousness with which they take the experimental task? willingness to admit to pathological behaviors? need to please the experimenter? socioeconomic status? and so forth. You should always keep in mind that when researchers rely on volunteers or convenience samples, such samples are biased in important ways, restricting the generalizability of the results; and this is true even if the researchers have randomly assigned these individuals to experimental conditions! Now, keeping these special concerns in mind, let's examine a fairly complicated experimental analogue study.

◆ PRELIMINARY EVALUATION

What Is the Structure of the Reasoning?

What are the issue and the conclusion?

> GENERAL ISSUE: What causes depression?
>
> SPECIFIC Issue: Do depressed people differ from nondepressed people in their subjective judgments of relations between behaviors and outcomes relative to the actual relations between behaviors and outcomes?
>
> CONCLUSION: Depressed people are more accurate than nondepressed people in judging the amount of control their responses exert over outcomes; depressed people are "sadder but wiser than nondepressed people." (empirical generalization)

Why do the issue and conclusion matter? In regard to the more general question, if we can determine major causes of depression we can design prevention and treatment programs. Regarding the more specific question, if we can get a clearer picture of how depressives make sense of the information in their environment, we can get a clearer picture of some of our major theories of depression.

What are the reasons? Research evidence: In two laboratory studies conducted by Alloy and Abramson, depressed students did not underestimate the degree of control their responses exerted over outcomes; in fact, they were accurate in these judgments. Instead, the nondepressed students revealed inaccuracies, believing themselves to have greater control or less control than was actually the case in different situations.

What terms or phrases are ambiguous?
"*Depressed persons.*" How depressed? Clinically depressed? Short-term depressed? Long-term?
"*Nondepressed persons.*" How typical?
"*More accurate.*" How accurate? Magnitude of effect?
"*Estimating the relationship between their actions and the outcome of situations.*" What relationships were they estimating? What kinds of judgments did they make?

What perspectives underlie the reasoning? The major theoretical perspective is cognitive theory, as illustrated by the emphasis on how people develop beliefs or cognitions about the relationships between their behavior and outcomes of situations. Psychological lenses that look inside us dominate over biological or sociocultural lenses, which would emphasize very different factors as the cause of depression.

◆ ADVANCED EVALUATION

Now, let's take a closer look at what Alloy and Abramson did in their laboratory project. They argue that the learned helplessness theory of depression provides both a strong and a weak prediction concerning how subjective beliefs about how our behaviors are related to environmental events (subjective contingencies) and how our behaviors are actually related to environmental events (objective contingencies). According to the strong prediction, depressed individuals should underestimate the degree of contingency between their responses and outcomes relative to the objective degree of contingency. That is, they should perceive less control over their world than they actually possess. According to the weak prediction, depressed individuals merely should judge that there is a smaller degree of contingency between their responses and outcomes than nondepressed individuals should.

To test these predictions, the researchers set up a task in which they could vary actual contingencies. The basic task in their studies was a series of trials in which subjects could either press or not press a button. Each trial had one of two outcomes. A green light was or was not turned on. The subjects were to try to turn on the green light by pressing the button. The actual degree of control a subject had could then be manipulated by the experimenter. For example, the experimenter could arrange for the green light to go on 75 percent of the time a subject pressed the button and 25 percent of the time that the button was not pressed. In this situation, the subject would be said to have 50 percent control (75 percent to 25 percent). After a series of trials, subjects would be asked to judge how much control they had had over the outcome.

In all experiments, subjects were paid undergraduate volunteers from the University of Pennsylvania. They were assigned to a depressed or nondepressed group on the basis of their Beck Depression Inventory (BDI) scores, a test commonly used to measure depression, which relies on responses to twenty-one self-report items, such as the following:

0	I do not feel sad.
1	I feel sad.
2	I am sad all the time and I can't snap out of it.
3	I am so sad or unhappy that I can't stand it.
0	I have not lost interest in other people.
1	I am less interested in other people than I used to be.
2	I have lost most of my interest in other people.
3	I have lost all of my interest in other people.

Subjects with BDI scores of 9 or above were assigned to the depressed group, and subjects scoring 8 or lower were assigned to the nondepressed group. The authors report much prior validity research on the BDI. For example, they report that correlations between BDI scores and clinically rated severity of depression in three studies were .65, .67, and .61, respectively, and that another study found that the BDI is a valid instrument for measuring depression in a college student population.

The researchers reported four experiments. In all studies, subjects were randomly assigned to the different experimental conditions. Prior to assignment, subjects filled out the BDI and another self-report measure of depression. After performing the experimental task, they completed several dependent variable measures. One was judgment of control; subjects rated the degree of control their responses (pressing and not pressing) exerted over the experimental outcome (green light onset). All subjects were given the following instructions: ". . . it is your task to learn what degree of control you have over whether or not this green light comes on," followed by detailed descriptions of the learning task. Following the task, subjects were asked to indicate their judgment of control by putting an "X" someplace on a scale that varied from 0 to 100. A second judgment scale was the judgment of total "reinforcement"; subjects estimated the overall percentage of trials on which green light onset occurred regardless of which response they made. On two other scales, subjects estimated the percentage of trials on which the green light came on when they pressed and when they did not press, respectively.

The focus here is on Experiments 2 and 3, which give us a good sense of the nature of their procedures and findings. The first experiment had demonstrated that subjects could learn to judge accurately the degree of relationship between their responses and outcomes in conditions in which pressing the button or not pressing the button was associated with various controls over the reinforcement.

In both Experiments 2 and 3, subjects had no control over the green light, but their perceptions of control varied as a function of experimental manipulations. In Experiment 2, Alloy and Abramson exposed depressed and nondepressed students to one of two situations. In one, the frequency with which the green light turned on was 75 percent and in the other it was 25 percent. Sixty-four subjects participated, half males and half females. Half were judged as depressed and half were judged as nondepressed. When the light turned on relatively infrequently—in only 25 percent of the trials—the depressed and nondepressed students did not significantly differ in their judgments of the degree of control they had had. The researchers report that both groups were relatively accurate and indicated that they had had little real control. But when the green light turned on frequently (75 percent), the nondepressed students markedly overestimated the degree of control they had had; depressed students did not. Table 1 summarizes the results for this study.

In Experiment 3 the investigators manipulated the consequences of turning on or not turning on the green light, while maintaining a situation in which subjects had no control over the reinforcement. Depressed and nondepressed students were put in one of two experimental situations. Subjects in one, the "lose" situation, were told that they were starting with 5 dollars and would lose 25 cents each time the light did not come on after they had pressed the button; in the other, the "win" situation, subjects started with no money but were told that they would win 25 cents each time the light came on after they had pressed the button. The money was to be given to the subjects at the conclusion of the study. In both situations, the light turned on following a button press 50 percent of the time and following a nonpress 50 percent of the time. Thus, subjects actually had no control. Again, 32 depressed and 32 nondepressed subjects participated. The authors report that both depressed and nondepressed students in the "lose" situation judged that they had had little control. But nondepressed students in the "win" situation greatly overestimated their degree of control. Table 2, on the next page, summarizes some of the actual data.

The authors state that Experiment 3 provided strong corroborative evidence for the hypothesis developed in Experiment 2: Depressed people accurately detect noncontingency between their responses and outcomes whereas nondepressed people show illusions of control, especially when they encounter pleasureful outcomes.

In summarizing all four of their experiments, Alloy and Abramson state: "Depressed students' judgments of contingency were surprisingly accurate in all four experiments. Nondepressed

TABLE 1 Means and Standard Deviations of Judged Control Scores by Problem, Mood, and Sex for Experiment 2

	NONDEPRESSED				DEPRESSED			
	MALES		FEMALES		MALES		FEMALE	
Problem	M	SD	M	SD	M	SD	M	SD
25–25	20.0	26.7	7.5	14.5	13.8	12.7	17.1	23.7
75–75	30.3	12.8	51.4	29.8	21.2	28.5	13.1	13.6

TABLE 2 **Means and Standard Deviations of Judged Control Scores by Problem, Mood, and Sex for Experiment 3**

	NONDEPRESSED				DEPRESSED			
	MALES		FEMALES		MALES		FEMALE	
Problem	M	SD	M	SD	M	SD	M	SD
Lose	6.9	11.9	21.2	8.8	21.2	20.3	11.4	13.1
Win	49.4	29.3	64.4	9.8	17.2	16.5	36.0	28.1

students, on the other hand, overestimated the degree of contingency between their responses and outcomes when noncontingent outcomes were frequent and/or desired and underestimated the degree of contingency when contingent outcomes were undesired. Thus, predictions derived from social psychology concerning the linkage between subjective and objective contingencies were confirmed for nondepressed students but not for depressed students. Further, the predictions of helplessness theory received, at best, minimal support."

The authors provide a revised learned helplessness theory on the basis of their results. The revised hypothesis maintains that depressives are characterized by a generalized expectation of no control, but postulates that this expectation only interferes with initiation of responses (the "motivational deficit" of helplessness) and not with the perception of response-outcome relationships (the "associative deficit" of helplessness). In other words, the revised helplessness hypothesis suggests that depressed individuals often perform poorly on instrumental tasks because they fail to generate the response that increases the probability of the successful outcome, not because they have trouble discerning the effect their responses exert on these outcomes.

Are depressed people sadder but wiser? Let's evaluate.

◆ ADVANCED EVALUATION

How Good Is the Evidence?

How generalizable is the sample?   Sample size is a major obstacle to generalization! In each study, group sample size is very small—8 in each of eight groups—and non-random. Many factors affecting whether college students volunteer for such a study may affect the results. The sample in each study lacks breadth on many important dimensions: age, geographical location, intelligence, and very importantly for the depressed groups, level of depression. The possible range of scores on BDI is 0 to 63; researchers labeled individuals as depressed who scored greater than 9, and the mean depression scores for depressed groups through the research tended to be below 15. How similar are college students who score in this range on the BDI to the clinically depressive individuals for whom we wish to generalize? Because of size, randomness, and breadth limitations, we would hesitate to generalize at all in this study, and would want to wait for other researchers to replicate with large, diverse, random samples.

How valid are the measures and the experimental manipulations? We need to ask about the validity of two key measures in these studies: judgment of contingency and judgment of depressed versus nondepressed. First, were the judgments of relationships between individuals' responses and environmental outcomes—judgments of control—in these laboratory tasks valid indicators of such judgments in the "real world"? For example, does my judgment of how much control I have over a green light in an experiment generalize to my judgment of how much control I have over events such as my future success with women, my salary, other people liking me, or my health? Can we assume that if depressive people seem "sadder but wiser" in learning relations between button presses and green-light outcomes, they will be sadder but wiser in learning the relationships between their real-life behaviors and real-life outcomes? We certainly would want to be cautious in drawing such a generalization.

How about a second important measure in the study—depression. The authors support their use of the BDI by referring to a number of earlier successful validation studies, providing some evidence of the validity of this measure. We do not know, however, how selective these references were, or how similar the sample in this study was to the samples used in the validation studies. Of greatest concern for generalization purposes is whether these college-student volunteers are analogous to people who might be given a clinical diagnosis of depression. The fact that most of the groups in this study averaged 15 or less on the BDI and also were sufficiently motivated to participate in classes and a research study suggests that they were not severely depressed as clinical populations.

Now, let's look closely at the validity of the manipulations in the two experiments that I have emphasized. In Experiment 2, the authors varied the percentage of time that people were reinforced (25 percent versus 75 percent of trials) but not the degree of control, which was always none. We need to ask, "Is this manipulation of the frequency of reinforcement for instrumental responses made in the lab analogous to the kinds of differences in the density of reinforcement that individuals experience for their responses in the real world?" In Experiment 3, the authors kept frequency of outcome (50 percent) and degree of control (again none) constant, but varied the value of the outcome: loss of a quarter when the green light did not come on versus gain of a quarter when the green light did come on. Thus, subjects either lost 5 dollars or won 5 dollars. It is questionable whether learning response-outcome relationships under these incentives in the lab is analogous to learning such relationships under typical incentives in the real world.

Are any statistics deceptive?   The researchers' emphasis on statistical differences can be somewhat deceptive, given the very large variability among scores and the very small sample size within each group. The magnitude of effect is not very large. For example, the standard deviations for the judgment of control measures of four of the eight groups in Experiment 2 and of three of the eight groups in Experiment 3 are greater than 20, suggesting much variability of scores and much overlap in scores among people in the different groups. The fact that the impact of the experimental manipulations varied markedly for people in the same condition suggests caution in generalizing. For example, although there is a big difference between depressed and nondepressed females in the 75–75 condition, there is also a huge standard deviation in the nondepressed females, suggesting that much of the difference may be due to a couple of very extreme scores.

Are there rival causes?   What hypotheses might account for the differences between depressed and nondepressed groups, other than differences in their depression levels? Is it possible that depressed people who volunteer are the types of individuals who are especially conscientious and thus would pay more attention to the experimental task? Do people who have a tendency to be depressed also have a tendency to be perfectionistic, and thus pay more attention to the task? A strength of this research is the authors' effort to address possible hypotheses through post-experimental interviews; interviews after Experiment 2 support a hypothesis to explain the differences. They revealed that the nondepressed subjects had a tendency to try more complex patterns of responding and to use non-logical reasoning in arriving at their judgments of control in the 75–75 problem, such as relying on "intuition" rather than logic, or relying on the percentage of reinforcements as an indicator of control.

What significant information is omitted? How many subjects in each group showed the illusion of control? How motivated were the subjects to perform well on this task? What were the motivations for volunteering? Would tasks other than button pressing depict relations between responses and outcomes and provide quite different results?

Have these results been replicated? What do other kinds of research studies tell us about how well depressed people process the information in their environment? Do they typically do so better than nondepressed people?

What conclusions are justified by the evidence? It is possible to set up conditions in the laboratory in which nondepressed people tend to be less realistic about their control over events than do depressed people, which is an interesting finding. However, it is an *overgeneralization* to state that depressed people *in general* are sadder but wiser. The small sample size, the artificiality of the task, and the questionable clinical depression in the subjects greatly restricts our ability to generalize.

Turning on the Transfer Switch

You should suspect you have encountered an experimental analogue study when:

1. The study took place in a laboratory or controlled setting.
2. Subjects in the study were animals or volunteer college students.
3. The experimenter manipulated a variable.

4. There is a major difference between what is done in the research setting and the complex social behavior to which we want to generalize.

Transfer Study
Phobic responses may be learned through imitating the reactions of others. The potential importance of observational learning in the developing of phobias is illustrated by a study by Mineka and others (1984). Adolescent rhesus monkeys were reared with parents who had an intense fear of snakes. During the observational learning sessions, the offspring saw their parents interact fearfully with real and toy snakes as well as nonfearfully with neutral objects. After six sessions, the fear of the adolescent monkeys was indistinguishable from that of the parents.

CHAPTER 10

General Issue: What Causes Abnormal Behavior?

Research Approach: Case-Control Procedure

Topic highlighted: Schizophrenia

Modern methods of producing images of brain activity have revealed evidence of structural abnormalities in the brains of schizophrenics, suggesting that brain defects may contribute to schizophrenia. Positron Emission Tomography (the PET) scan provides information about the metabolic processes of the brain, that is, the brain's use of oxygen. The faster the metabolic rate, the higher the level of brain activity. PET scans of the brains of schizophrenics find lower than normal metabolic rates in the frontal lobes and basal ganglia (Buchsbaum and Haier, 1987; Buchsbaum et al., 1982). These areas are involved in the regulation of attention, so these findings are consistent with psychological evidence of deficits in attention among schizophrenics.

Our opening passage illustrates one of the most common strategies psychologists use to determine the causes of abnormal behavior: comparing people diagnosed with some disorder (e.g., schizophrenia) with people not diagnosed with that disorder (a control group) regarding some characteristic that a researcher believes might be a cause of that disorder (e.g., brain metabolism). This design has been termed the *case-control procedure* because a group of cases (e.g., persons with the diagnosis of interest, such as schizophrenia) is compared to an appropriate control group (such as hospitalized depressives) regarding some characteristic. Usually, if the two groups differ significantly in having this characteristic, then the researcher infers that the characteristic is a cause of the disorder. For example, our sample textbook passage reasons that because research found that brains of schizophrenics had lower than normal metabolic rates, this strengthens the view that brain defects may contribute to schizophrenia. The use of the phrase "lower than normal" suggests the presence of a normal control group, and the use of the phrase "may contribute" implies a causal conclusion.

This widely applied research strategy can easily fool us, because the presence of a control group makes it look like an experimental study. It is not such a study, however; it is just a special form of a correlational study which we discussed in our last chapter. Why is that? Because the researcher does not experimentally manipulate, or randomly assign subjects to any condition of interest (for example, schizophrenia). Instead, participants *bring with them* whatever it is that the researcher is interested in studying. Because of that, the control group doesn't really control very much; it always *differs from the group with the disorder by having many characteristics* other than the one that interests the researcher. That is, the design does not isolate the characteristic of interest from other possible causes. This research strategy possesses unique concerns of which you want to be aware. Let's examine several, then evaluate the study on which our opening passage is based.

1. *Failure to reveal direction and nature of relation of the two variables.* Because no experimentally manipulated independent variable actually exists in this design (although researchers will often label their variables as independent and dependent variables), we must raise questions about just how the variables in the study should affect one another and concern ourselves with the *direction of causation.* For example, is the disorder a cause of the characteristic of interest? (e.g., is schizophrenia a cause of a metabolic disturbance in the brain?), is the characteristic of interest a cause of the disorder? (is a metabolic disturbance a cause of the schizophrenic disorder?), are some other factors causing the relation between the disorder and the characteristic of interest? (e.g., is a form of stress a cause both of a metabolic dis-

turbance and schizophrenic symptoms?) or do the disorder and the characteristic of interest influence each other? We advance the critical thinking process by reflecting upon the direction of cause.
2. *High variability of behavior within research groups and large overlap of behavior between groups.* Researchers using this design usually report statistical test results showing that the *means* of the groups studied did or did not differ significantly. Even when group means differ significantly in a *statistical* sense, individual behavior can vary greatly within groups, and often the behaviors of the most disturbed group vary more than those of the control groups. Thus, distributions of behaviors often greatly overlap, which means that many people in the "case" group share behavioral characteristics with many people in the "control" group. Frequently, the amount of overlap is such that large groups of cases and controls are indistinguishable. That is, if we know someone's value relative to the characteristic of interest (e.g., metabolic rate), then we cannot accurately predict to which group that person belongs.

An example should help us better appreciate the meaning and relevance of overlap. A researcher hypothesized that one aspect of the schizophrenic's disorder is a relative impairment in the ability to think abstractly. Using a measure of abstract thinking, in which the higher the score, the better the abstract thinking, he found the following results:

	MEANS	STANDARD DEVIATION
Normals:	33.05	2.72
Schizophrenics	30.49	3.70

The means differed significantly. However, there is considerable overlap, in that *33 percent of the patients scored above the normal group's mean, and 25 percent of the normals scored below the schizophrenic group mean.* When many individuals in the disorder group score the same or better than those in the control group, then we have extensive overlap. In addition, the standard deviation of 3.70 shows that *schizophrenics differed greatly from each other,* a common finding in case-control research. It should be clear from this data that if we knew anyone's individual value on the abstract thinking task, we could not predict very well whether that person was schizophrenic. Note that if a characteristic were truly caused by a disorder or were the major cause of a disorder, then overlap would not be expected. For example, if we compare people with mononucleosis with people who have no physical illness, most of the normals will show a different white cell count than most of those with the illness; there will be very little overlap.

Thus, when research evidence shows extensive overlap between case and control groups, we should be wary of how impressed we should be by the data. Extensive overlap signifies a weak relationship, and often such weak findings can be explained by other causes than those hypothesized by the researcher. As a general rule, the greater the overlap, the more likely that differences can be accounted for by uncontrolled rival causes. Because of this, we should not treat evidence showing extensive overlap between case and control groups as very persuasive.

3. *Hidden variables.* Perhaps the most important concern when critically evaluating studies comparing case and control groups is that the groups will always differ from one another regarding numerous characteristics other than the one of primary interest to the researcher. Some of these *pre-existing differences* may contribute to the difference between the groups. Such pre-existing differences are important rival causes for us to consider. Following are several common possible rival causes of differences between groups.

   a. *Socioeconomic status* and variables associated with differences in class, such as nutrition, learning opportunities, exposure to chemicals, cognitive abilities, parental conflict patterns, prenatal care, and parental stimulation.

   b. *Drug use.* Often, individuals diagnosed with disorders will differ from people without disorders because of greater use of drugs.

   c. *Patienthood and hospitalization.* Hospitalization affects people in ways that are likely to affect their performance in a research study. For example, individuals in a patient role relate to authorities, such as researchers, in very different ways than those not in that role. To appreciate the magnitude of hospitalization as a variable, we can contemplate how we personally might be different in important ways after spending several years in a hospital setting.

When we encounter a study that adopts the case-control strategy, we always want to ask, "In what ways do these groups differ?" We will frequently discover rival causes to account for the researcher's findings.

Careful researchers anticipate this concern and try to correct for it by trying to *match groups* on as many characteristics as they can. Matching groups on characteristics means that the researcher tries to select groups who are as similar to each other as possible on characteristics that we might expect to influence behavior. Thus, for example, if the "cases" have been hospitalized for a year for some disorder, then researchers will select controls that have been hospitalized for a year with a different disorder, perhaps a medical disorder, if the researchers believe that hospitalization is an important influence on the characteristics of interest. The more thorough the matching, the more confidence we can have in the researchers' hypothesis.

4. *Common sampling biases.* Generalizing from samples in case-control studies is especially precarious because of a number of common *sampling biases.* Let's note some of these.

a. *Prior treatment history.* Individuals who have been treated differ from untreated cases (that is, diagnosable persons in the community with no treatment history) in important ways; thus we cannot generalize from treated to untreated cases. For example, long-term drug treatment, hospitalization, or psychotherapy may greatly influence treated cases in relation to many characteristics.

b. *Differences in institutions.* Patients admitted to a state hospital can be expected to differ from those admitted to a private hospital in ways that may affect the study results. For example, they may differ on socio-economic status, education, and income, all of which are potentially important influences on research results.

c. *Duration of disorder and number of prior treatment contacts.* The length of time individuals have experienced a disorder and the number of times individuals have been treated may affect how they respond to research. For example, patients who have many prior treatment contacts may differ markedly from first-admission cases, that is, those who are being treated for the first time on important characteristics such as presence of psychotic symptoms and adaptation to their disorder.

d. *Subjects' willingness to consent.* Subjects who are willing to participate in a research study may differ markedly from those who are not. For example, they may be more highly motivated, more dependent on authority figures, and more trusting of researchers.

5. *Uncertainty of retrospective reporting.* When this method is used to study the early antecedents of a disorder, a major difficulty is the error involved in retrospective reporting. Reports of the past have been shown to be importantly biased in many ways. For example, individuals who have disorders may distort past events in ways that may help explain their current problems to them.

Because of all of these potential biases, we need to be very alert to how subjects were selected when we evaluate case-control studies. Now, let's critically evaluate our opening passage, applying some of these specific concerns within the context of our critical questions.

◆ PRELIMINARY ANALYSIS

What is the Reasoning Structure?

What are the issue and the conclusion?
GENERAL ISSUE: What causes schizophrenia?

SPECIFIC ISSUE: Do brain abnormalities cause schizophrenia?

CONCLUSION: Brain defects may contribute to schizophrenia (explanation).

Why do the issue and conclusion matter? Schizophrenia is one of our most serious, and least understood, disorders. If we can discover some of its causes, we may eventually be able to discover how to prevent and cure the disorder.

What are the reasons?
EVIDENCE: Schizophrenics differ from normals in metabolic rates in the frontal lobes; these differences coincide with evidence of deficits in attention in schizophrenics (empirical generalizations).

SUPPORT FOR GENERALIZATION: PET scans show that schizophrenics have lower levels of brain activity than normal controls (not further specified).

What terms or phrases are ambiguous?
"Lower than normal metabolic rates." How much lower? Is there much overlap in measures between normals and schizophrenics? *"Findings coincide with psychological evidence of deficits in attention."* Is there a strong association?

What perspectives underlie the reasoning?   Biological.

◆ DETAILED LOOK AT THE STUDY

Now, let's critically evaluate the research, having available specific information about procedures. Our opening passage references two major sources, an article that summarizes a number of studies (Buchsbaum and Haier, 1987) and an article that reports an original research study in detail (Buchsbaum et al., 1982). Our focus is on the original research study, because it is typical of those studies reported in Buchsbaum and Haier's summary report, and the issues we raise with it can also be raised with other studies addressing this research question.

Researchers studied eight schizophrenic patients, two women and six men (age range, 18 to 29 years), who were inpatients at the National Institutes of Health (NIH) Clinical Center, Bethesda, Maryland. Patients had the following characteristics: all had been receiving medications for at least two weeks; all except one were right-handed; all were judged to be in good physical health; one had a history of head injury; none had clinically significant brain abnormalities that were evident from physical examination or laboratory tests. Control subjects were four men and two women who were volunteers from the hospital, and were described as being staff or college students. All were healthy according to their medical histories, and neither they nor their first-degree relatives had psychiatric histories.

Diagnoses were based on both DSM-III and Research Diagnostic Criteria (RDC) applied by the patient's psychiatrist and were confirmed by another staff psychiatrist. Also, when they used a different diagnostic system, based on another definition of schizophrenia, six of the eight patients were judged as having a high probability for the diagnosis of schizophrenia, and two patients were judged as probably schizophrenic. None had a family history for schizophrenia.

The primary measure of interest was the local cerebral uptake of deoxyglucose, which was measured by Positron Emission Tomography (PET). This measurement procedure is quite complicated, but its final product is a computer image that provides information about the metabolic processes of the brain, that is, the brain's use of oxygen. The faster the metabolic rate, the higher the level of brain activity. Researchers reported that the mean (both right and left) anterior cortical segment whole-slice ratio was 1.12 (standard deviation = .05) in normal subjects and 1.06 (standard deviation = .04) in schizophrenic patients, which they reported as a significant difference. They concluded that this indicates that schizophrenics show relatively lower glucose use than normal control subjects, a finding consistent with previously reported studies of regional cerebral blood flow. The researchers cautioned that their findings were preliminary.

◆ ADVANCED EVALUATION

How Good Is the Evidence?

How generalizable are the samples? Sample size is very small, and we cannot tell whether these subjects were randomly selected from any larger population because the researchers fail to inform us of how these particular schizophrenics ended up being the subjects in this study. Selective biases are probably strongly operative in both groups. The sample does have some breadth in regard for important dimensions: severity of disorder, premorbid functioning and duration of illness, and presence of psychoses.

How valid are the measures and the manipulations? The researchers do not experimentally manipulate schizophrenia or brain metabolic activity. They measure them both, creating two measurement validity issues. First, can we be confident that individuals labeled as schizophrenic are appropriately categorized? Diagnoses were completed in a thorough, careful manner, and two psychiatrists agreed on the judgment. Our confidence in the generalizability of the schizophrenia diagnoses depends upon our confidence in the diagnostic wisdom of psychiatrists working at the Bethesda, Maryland, NIH Clinical Center. We should keep in mind that diagnosticians in one setting often disagree with those in other settings about what criteria to use to diagnose schizophrenia.

Measuring cerebral metabolism is a very complex process. Those of us not closely associated with the technique cannot adequately judge its merit; we must rely on the experts. Even so, we can check the research for reliability information; and in this case, the researcher reports very high reliability of the measures. This means that the measures provide repeatable findings, increasing the likelihood of validity. This measure makes sense to us. We have no good reason to doubt that the measure indexes brain metabolism; thus, we can apply the principle of charity and adopt a working assumption that this measure is a valid index of brain metabolic activity.

Are there rival causes?   There are many possibilities. The question we want to ask is, "What might account for the differences in metabolic activity found between the two groups?" I have listed some possibilities. Can you add some more?

1. Might schizophrenics react quite differently to testing conditions than normals, causing differences in PET measures?

2. Were there observer expectancy effects? Buchsbaum et al. fail to specify whether those collecting measurements had any clues about whether the slides came from schizophrenic versus normal participants.

3. Could the differences found be an effect of the cumulative effects of schizophrenia, not its cause?

4. Could the differences found be due to the long-term effects of medication?

5. Might the differences found be due to effects associated with social class, which tends to be lower in schizophrenics? Such associated effects include nutritional and exercise habits, exposure to lead, and so forth, all of which might affect brain metabolism.

6. Could the differences reflect impairment only in certain subgroups of schizophrenics, such as hospitalized schizophrenics? If there are many schizophrenias, as some argue, then maybe

there is something unique about this group that is not true of other schizophrenics.

Are any statistics deceptive?   We should note the *magnitude* of the effect. The groups do show some overlap, indicating that *some* schizophrenics show levels higher than *some* normals.

What significant information is omitted?   Have other researchers replicated the findings by using different populations of individuals with schizophrenic disorders? How long had these patients been hospitalized? How long had they been on drugs prior to being taken off drugs for the study? How were the patients selected for the study? How experienced were the psychiatrists making the diagnoses? What human behaviors are these brain structures related to? Are other brain structures potentially more important? Is this reduction of brain activity unique to schizophrenics, or also typical of other disorders, such as bipolar affective disorders? What do other indexes of brain activity show?

What conclusion is justified by the evidence?   Because of the small, probably highly biased, samples and the feasibility of many rival hypotheses, these findings are thought-provoking but very inconclusive. But, as the researchers themselves note, they are preliminary. They serve as stimulation for further research and need to be replicated across diverse settings and samples. (Note: Buchsbaum and Haier's 1987 paper reviews replication attempts.)

Turning on the Transfer Switch

Cues: Two features that should alert you to the presence of case-control studies are: (a) presence of *reports of differences* in characteristics between "disordered" and "well" groups (e.g., schizophrenics versus "normals"), or between different kinds of disorders (e.g., schizophrenic disorders versus bipolar affective disorders); and (b) absence of an experimental manipulation. Characteristics researchers commonly study include:

1.   Childhood experiences (e.g., abuse, loss of parent, family discipline, etc.)

2. Amount or kinds of recent life stress
3. Family communication patterns and emotional reactivity
4. Presence or absence of birth trauma or injury
5. Biochemistry (e.g., dopamine or serotonin levels)
6. Performance (e.g., attention span, reaction time, achievement tests, etc.)

Transfer Study
Are stressful life events an important cause of depression? A study by Brown and Harris (1978) addresses this question. Brown and Harris interviewed 114 women who were being treated for depression and a random sample of 458 women who were living in the community; they divided these women into those who showed clear symptoms of depression during the interview and those who did not. All of the women were asked about the occurrence of stressful events, particularly during the past year. The researchers found an increased incidence of stressful events among the depressed patients, but only with regard to a particular subset of such events—those that were severe and that involved long-term consequences for the woman's wellbeing. Two such prominent events were divorce and marital separation. Sixty-one percent of the depressed patients had experienced such an event in the nine months preceding the onset of their symptoms; only 25 percent of the women in the community sample had experienced an event of this nature in the nine months prior to their interview. These results suggest that the experience of a severe event with long-term consequences is one important cause of depression.

CHAPTER 11

♦

General Issue: What Causes Abnormal Behavior?

Research Approach: Twin Studies

Topic highlighted: Schizophrenia

Is schizophrenia inherited? To address this question, Gottesman and Shields (1972) compared concordance rates for schizophrenia in monozygotic (MZ) and dizygotic (DZ) twins. They located 55 patients who were consensually diagnosed as schizophrenic, were twins, and had a twin who could be located and would cooperate in the study. Of these, zygostity determination yielded 22 MZ and 33 DZ twin pairs. Using psychological, medical, and social data to diagnose each twin pair, Gottesman and Shields found a big difference in concordance rates: 50 percent of MZ twins and 9 percent of DZ twins were concordant for schizophrenia. These results, in conjunction with many other studies that have found concordance rates for MZ twins higher than for DZ twins, strongly suggest a genetic basis for schizophrenia.

Is schizophrenia inherited? Is it in our genes? If my parents are schizophrenic, will I be? Sorting out genetic from environmental causes has a long history in the field of abnormal psychology. One strategy investigators frequently use is the *twin-study strategy*. This strategy provides interesting, but difficult to interpret, data. Examining this study should be of special interest to us because researchers have used the same data from such studies to support beliefs in both environmental and in genetic causes of disorders. The logic of twin studies is as follows. Identical twins are monozygotic (MZ)—they result from the fertilization of a single ovum. An extra split of the zygote early in development results in the birth of two *genetically identical* individuals, always of the same sex, and almost always of identical appearance. Dizygotic (DZ) twins occur when two separate sperm fertilize two separate ova at about the same time; the two are no more alike genetically than are ordinary siblings, and share on average about 50 percent of their genes; also their physical resemblance is no greater than that of ordinary siblings. If schizophrenia is caused *solely* by a single gene or combination of genes, then if one twin develops schizophrenia, the other (the co-twin) also should develop it—a 100% concordance rate, a rate that should be much higher than the concordance rate for DZ twins. Also, if one is *predisposed* (or vulnerable) to schizophrenia because of an inherited gene, such that interaction with certain environmental factors activates the predisposition causing schizophrenia, then MZ twins should have a concordance rate less than 100%, but a rate much higher than for DZ twins.

The major logical problem with twin studies is that MZ twins, who typically resemble one another strikingly in appearance, are treated much more similarly than are DZs by others, such as their parents and peers, and this similarity can also account for differences in concordance. For example, MZ twins tend to spend more time with each other, doing similar things, than DZ twins. They are also more likely to dress similarly, to play together, and to have the same friends.

Let me give you some clues to help you further see why separating genetic and environmental factors is so difficult in twin studies. Let's assume that a researcher is interested in using twin studies to sort out genetic and environmental contributions to whether someone develops leadership qualities. So she locates students in college who have such qualities and are also twins. She then finds their co-twins, some who are identical, some who are not. She discovers that the concordance rate for leadership is 50% in the MZ twins and only 15% in the DZ twins, results which on the surface seem to support a major genetic contribution to leadership. But what do these results prove? Well, first they suggest that something these MZ twins have in common facilitates a leadership development process. But what is it they have in common, and what is the process?

There are many possibilities. That's why drawing conclusions is so difficult. For example, perhaps the age at which one develops into adolescent maturity influences the likelihood of one becoming a leader. For example, early-maturing, more than late-maturing boys, are likely to be accorded more popularity, prestige, or leadership roles by their peers. Rate of maturity is associated with genetic and nutritional factors. In this case, the genetically related early-body maturation influences the leadership role only because in our particular culture adults and peers react to early maturers by giving them responsibilities usually given to older persons. Also, if one MZ twin tends to exhibit early maturation, so will the other. DZ twins will be much less similar in their maturation process. Thus, concordance rates of leadership behavior would be expected to differ.

So, how much of this concordance difference can we say is due to genes and how much is due to the environment? Can you see that the question doesn't make much sense? In our example, the gene for early maturation *predisposes* one toward leadership roles, but such a role cannot develop unless those in the culture respond selectively. Thus, both genetic and environmental factors mutually influence each other. Consequently, sorting out genetic from environmental causes in such cases is much like examining a previously baked brownie and deciding how much of its "browniness" is due to sugar, water, flour, and the heat of the oven. It would be impossible to reverse the baking process in such a way that we could see how each of these factors contributed to the brownie. All the factors mutually affect each other, but we cannot know how they do this by breaking the finished brownie down into each of its elements. That is a major difficulty with twin studies. They can tell us that genetic and environmental factors are important, but not *how* they influence behavior. Thus, we have to be very careful in interpreting the results of twin studies, and we will want to be especially alert to *rival causes* to explain discrepancies in concordance rates. Often these causes will be complex interactions between gene determined physical and biological characteristics and cultural reactions to these characteristics.

In addition to the problem of sorting out genetic from environmental factors, we should be sensitive to some other problems in twin-study research. Let's examine another important one—the problem of validly determining whether twins are indeed MZ or DZ and whether they have similar disorders.

Sometimes it is not a simple matter to tell whether a co-twin is or is not identical. For example, co-twins of index cases (the ones we start with) are often dead or unavailable for personal examination. Thus, researchers often must make informed guesses about whether a given pair is MZ or DZ, and whether the co-twin has the same disorder. If the same person makes the guesses, it opens the way for *expectancy effects* to bias the diagnoses. Thus, we should always ask how "blind" investigators are to the determination of zygosity and the diagnosis of the co-twin.

Sometimes researchers may have independent judges make blind diagnoses using written case histories. Such case histories, however, contain selective material gathered and prepared by other investigators who perhaps were not themselves "blind." Now, keeping some of these concerns in mind, let's do a preliminary evaluation of our opening twin-study passage.

◆ PRELIMINARY EVALUATION

What Is the Structure of the Reasoning?

What are the issue and conclusion?

GENERAL ISSUE: What is the cause of schizophrenia?

SPECIFIC ISSUE: Does schizophrenia have a genetic cause?

CONCLUSION: Yes, schizophrenia has a genetic etiology.

What are the reasons?
MZ twins have a higher concordance rate for schizophrenia than do DZ twins (research generalization).

Support for generalization: 50% of MZ twins and 9% of DZ twins were concordant for schizophrenia.

Why do the issue and conclusion matter?
This issue has theoretical importance for helping us understand schizophrenia. For example, if we can discover genetic or environmental determinants, we may be able to determine better treatments or do further research to pinpoint reasons for the differences.

What terms or phrases are ambiguous?
"Variety of psychological, medical, and social data." Exactly what procedures were used to determine the diagnoses made?
"Consistent with other studies." How consistent? How many studies?
"Genetic basis." What do they mean by this; for example, how do genes influence the disorder? Do they predispose?

What perspectives underlie the reasoning? Biological. The researcher is interested in genes as causes.

◆ ADVANCED EVALUATION

Further important details of the study are as follows. Researchers sampled schizophrenic twins from the Maudsley Hospital twin register, which attempts to record a complete, uninterrupted series of twins, defined as those (1) who were born one of a multiple birth, and (2) whose co-twin was of the same sex as the patient and survived until the age of five in the case of Children's Department patients, or age fifteen in the case of adults. The Maudsley and Bethlem Royal Joint Hospital is a postgraduate teaching hospital, exclusively for psychiatry. The Maudsley population from which the twins were obtained consisted largely of outpatients. Two-thirds of referrals of outpatients come from general practitioners, and of these, 70% are from general practitioners in south London. The second largest source of outpatients is self-referrals (18%), also mostly local.

A total of 392 twins with various psychiatric diagnoses were identified from Maudsley Hospital from consecutive admissions from 1948 to 1964, 47 of whom had at some time been diagnosed at the hospital as suffering from schizophrenia. The 47 twins consisted of 22 males and 25 females. After excluding 6 of these for various reasons and adding 21 cases discovered to have been diagnosed as schizophrenic after their discharge from the hospital, the final number of schizophrenic probands included became 62, 31 males and 31 females. Of these, 28 probands had MZ co-twins and 34 had DZ co-twins. Since 4 MZ pairs and 1 DZ pair were represented by two twins, both meeting the defined criteria for being included, the 62 probands came from 57 pairs (24 MZs, 13 males; 33 DZs, 17 males). The researchers noted that the sample had a higher representation of cases with a good prognosis because they sampled consecutive admissions to an outpatient service. There was an even split for sex among the probands. The median age was 37, with a range from 19 to 64.

Zygosity was determined as follows: blood grouping and fingerprinting (16 pairs), blood grouping only (15 pairs), fingerprinting only (5 pairs), twins seen by same observer (11 pairs), a history of difference in appearance without direct observational confirmation (10 pairs).

Information for diagnoses varied and included background and further information as was already recorded in the Maudsley Hospital charts or Genetics Unit files, interviews, personality inventories, and some correspondence by mail. Twins were interviewed by the researchers wherever they happened to be living at the time. Investigators summarized all their information in a case study summary. The summaries did not refer to the zygosity of the pair or to the diagnosis, if any, of the co-twin. The summary was given to six judges who were blind to whether the twins were MZ or DZ and blind to the diagnoses of the co-twin. All 114 summaries were diagnosed by each of six judges of different backgrounds from the United Kingdom, United States, and Japan. Judges were free to pursue diagnoses as they wished and were asked to make a diagnosis that could be classified as: S, or schizophrenia; ?S, or uncertain schizophrenia; O, other psychiatric anomaly; and N, standing for normal, or within normal limits. The six judges voted unanimously on 58 of 114 cases, and 43 other cases had no more than 2 minority votes. The remaining 13 twins, all with 3 or more S votes and none with less than 3, were classified as S. Twins with an accumulation of at least 3 S or ?S votes were called ?S. The frequency of diagnoses of schizophrenia among the six judges ranged from 43 to 77. The average agreement by the six judges across all 144 twins was 79.4%.

After losing two MZ pairs from the sample who did not meet the criteria of the six-judge diagnostic panel, researchers found pairwise concordance rates of 50% (11–22) in MZ and 9% (3/33) in DZ pairs for definite or probable schizophrenia. When stricter criteria were used to determine the diagnosis, rates dropped to 40% and 10%. The researchers conclude the following on the basis of the above evidence and much other evidence that they consider in their book: Genetic factors specific to schizophrenia are conclusively involved in its etiology. They also state that this does not imply that genetic factors are the only ones involved.

◆ ADVANCED EVALUATION

How Good Is the Evidence?

How generalizable is the sample? The proportion of all hospital patients who are MZ and DZ twins matches quite closely the proportion in the general population, suggesting that there was not a biased tendency for twins to be referred to the hospital. Also, the percentage of twins diagnosed as schizophrenic matches the percentage of all Maudsley patients so diagnosed. This suggests that there was not a significant excess of schizophrenic twins, which we might expect if such twins were referred to the hospital because they were cases of special research or teaching interest, or if twins per se were especially susceptible to schizophrenia. Also, the sample size of MZ and DZ schizophrenic probands was quite large.

A major issue is whether the types of schizophrenics who are referred to this hospital are representative of schizophrenics in the general population. After all, these MZ schizophrenics form but a small proportion of all possible schizophrenics, and schizophrenic disorder is a very heterogeneous one. Because the sample of schizophrenic twins is not a random selection of schizophrenics in England, selective factors that led these particular types of schizophrenics to Maudsley may bias the results.

The sample lacks geographical breadth, and our summarized description provides insufficient information to determine distribution across socioeconomic class, intelligence, and kinds of schizophrenic symptoms. Because the definitions of schizophrenia continue to change over time, we do not know how the diagnoses in this study match, for example, the diagnoses that would be made using DSM-III, which uses much stricter criteria than prior diagnostic systems. Thus, we have to be cautious in how broadly we generalize.

How valid are the measures and the experimental manipulations?
Two measures are of special interest: determination of zygosity and of the psychiatric diagnosis. The researchers used a variety of procedures for determining zygosity. Bias is most likely in those cases

seen by the same observer—if the observer knew whether the twins were concordant for schizophrenia—and in cases determined by a history of difference in appearance. Thus, there is some possibility of misclassification of zygosity, but it is unlikely that the frequency of errors would greatly affect the results.

Diagnosing individuals as having a schizophrenic disorder is a subjective, complex process. A strength of the study is its use of consensus among diverse judges for the diagnoses. Although judges varied markedly in their willingness to label an individual as schizophrenic, they showed good overall agreement with one another in diagnosing. Whether patients diagnosed as schizophrenic truly had a schizophrenic disorder cannot be determined, because no infallible criterion exists for making such a judgment. Procedures used to make diagnoses were quite thorough, and judges making the diagnoses came from diverse backgrounds. Thus, we should have some confidence that other groups of judges would have made similar judgments, at least judges making diagnoses at a similar point in time. Thus, we should have some confidence in the reliability of these judgments; however, we must still reserve judgment on the validity of the diagnosis. The effort to have judges blind to whether the co-twin was MZ or DZ and whether the co-twin was schizophrenic strengthens the generalizability of the judgments. However, we should not be surprised to see some biases creeping into the case summary write-ups given to the judges.

Are there rival causes?   Some rival causes are:
1. The environments of MZ twins are more similar than environments of DZ twins, because the common appearance leads people to respond to the MZ twins more similarly than to the DZ twins.
2. Researchers, knowing about both twins when they made up summaries to be used by judges to make their diagnoses, let their biases creep into the summaries.
3. Interviewers making diagnoses from the researchers' summaries picked up subtle cues about zygosity, and these biased their judgments.

Are any statistics deceptive?   Not really. The pairwise concordance rates can be a little misleading because they are percentages based on a rather small frequency. However, the researchers report both frequencies and percentages, which permits the reader to consider both.

What significant information is omitted?   What definition of schizophrenia were these judges using? How do these definitions compare to modern day definitions? How consistent are these findings with other comparisons of MZ and DZ twins? or with results from other research approaches, such as adoption studies?

What conclusions are justified by the evidence?   We can't conclude from this study or from any twin study that schizophrenia is *caused* by genetic factors. We can conclude that given the definition of schizophrenia and the diagnostic procedures used by these investigators, the concordance rate of schizophrenia is higher in monozygotic than in dizygotic twins, and that this is certainly suggestive that genetic factors play a role in the development of schizophrenic disorders. But what that role is, we cannot know from this research. We can't draw any conclusions about how biological, psychological, and sociocultural factors interact to account for the development of schizophrenic symptoms. For example, even with a high MZ concordance rate for schizophrenia, it is quite possible that the major determinant of whether someone develops schizophrenia is a cultural response to some biological characteristic.

We want to remember that the diagnostic criteria for schizophrenia shift greatly over time, greatly affecting concordance rates. We also should remind ourselves that even if it is true that genes influence biological mechanisms that in turn influence the likelihood of a schizophrenic disorder, we can't conclude that the most effective treatment for schizophrenia is a biologically based treatment, such as the use of drugs.

For example, behavioral and insight oriented psychotherapies may have an influence on behavior even if one of the contributing causes to the behavior is genetic. The treatment of headaches illustrates this logic. For many people who seem to have a biological predisposition to headaches, relaxation training, a behavioral technique, can be quite effective. The major point to remember is that psychologically oriented interventions can have important influences on biologically influenced behavior.

Remember: it is probably the case that understanding schizophrenic disorders is going to require us to have a good understanding of how predisposing, precipitating, and reinforcing causal factors interact.

Turning on the Transfer Switch

Genetic factors implicated in alcoholism! Depression is in our genes! Panic disorders are inherited! Gene found for manic-depressive disorder! All around us today are claims about genetic causes of disorders. Such claims are likely to be accompanied by references to twin-study research. It should be pretty easy for you to recognize situations in which individuals are using twin studies in their arguments. Look for references for comparisons between MZ and DZ twins.

Transfer Study
A predisposition toward Attention-Deficit Hyperactivity Disorder is probably inherited. Researchers studied over 200 twin pairs and found that the concordance for clinically diagnosed hyperactivity was 51 percent for identical twins and only 33 percent for fraternal twins.

CHAPTER 12

◆━━━━━━━━━━━━━━━━━━━━━━━━━━━━━━━

General Issue: What Causes Abnormal Behavior?

Research Approach: Adoption Studies

Topic highlighted: Schizophrenia

One way to sort out the contribution of genetic and environmental factors is to compare the rates of schizophrenia in children who have been adopted and raised by normal foster parents but who have biological parents who did or did not have schizophrenia. An early study of this type examined 49 individuals whose mothers suffered from schizophrenia and 53 whose mothers did not (Heston, 1966). Results indicated that among the persons whose biological mothers had schizophrenia, 11 percent developed schizophrenia, but among those whose biological mothers were normal, none developed schizophrenia. Results of this study provide strong evidence of a genetic basis for schizophrenia.

As mentioned in our previous chapter, a major logical problem with twin studies is that MZ twins, who typically resemble one another strikingly in appearance, are treated much more similarly than are DZs by parents and peers. Thus differences in concordance rates between MZs and DZs may be due to a greater similarity of environmental circumstances among MZs. Because of this flaw, many investigators have turned to adoption studies to try to better separate genetic from environmental factors. Such studies try to control for the possible effects of differences in environmental circumstances.

Researchers apply several different adoption strategies, but the one with the longest history and the one we can learn a great deal from is the one depicted in our opening passage—often called the *adoptees design*—a procedure that attempts to keep the environments comparable, but the genetic contributions different. The first step of this strategy is to identify adoptees with one biological parent—usually the mother—who is affected with the disorder of interest. The second step is to identify a control group of adoptees whose parents are not affected with the disorder. To best separate genetic and environmental influences, only adoptees who were separated from their biological parents very soon after birth and who were adopted into the homes of non-relatives should be included in the study. The last step is to assess and diagnose adoptees of the two groups, while remaining blind to the status of their biological parentage. If children of *mothers with a disorder* have a higher rate of the disorder than children of *mothers not having the disorder*, then the difference should be due to the inherited genes. This reasoning makes sense, if indeed there is no systematic difference between the two groups of adoptees in their adoptive environments that might be relevant to the development of the disorder—a big if!

As with twin studies, we need to be especially alert to the following question when we evaluate adoption studies: "What are the rival causes?" The most important assumption made in such studies is that the environments of the two groups of adoptees—on the average—are the same. However, *selective placement by adoption agencies*, such as placing the offspring of psychiatric patients into less fit adoptive families than the offspring of non-psychiatric families may lead to systematic differences in the environment; and it would not be surprising if the adoption process were subject to such biases. For example, in one well-known study, researchers found that in 8 of 24 adoptive families of schizophrenic adoptees, an adoptive parent had been in a mental hospital, which was not true of a single adoptive parent of a control adoptee. Thus, an important rival cause for explaining differences in rates of disorders in adoption studies may be *selective placement*.

Another difficulty in explaining the results of adoption studies is that we inherit characteristics that affect how our environment is going to respond to us; we enter the world with physical characteristics and temperaments that in part create the environment that influences us. Thus, while differences between adoptee groups may suggest that *something* genetic is going on, they don't tell us how much of the behavioral outcome (e.g., a psychiatric disorder) is due to what children bring to their environment and how much is due to the complex interaction between genetic and environmental factors. As in our discussion of twin studies, let's examine a hypothetical example. If we begin our lives with a low activity-level temperament (highly gene determined), we will create an environment for ourselves that will lead to different outcomes than if we enter the world with a high activity level. For example, people might want to spend less time with us because we are so apathetic and this leads us to feel badly about ourselves. If the interaction between activity level and the environment increases the likelihood that we will develop some disorder, how much of the cause of that disorder is genetic? How much is environmental? We cannot tell! Thus, twin studies and adoption studies that find results consistent with genetic-cause hypotheses can tell us that something of genetic importance is probably happening. What they cannot tell us directly is to what extent a disorder is caused by genetic versus environmental influences.

Another general concern related to interpretations from adoption studies is that only certain biological parents give up or are permitted to give up their children for legal adoption. Thus, when we examine children of schizophrenic mothers, we do not have a random sample of such mothers. It is difficult to assess how this selective factor affects the findings. A further difficulty is generalizing from the sample of adopting parents; they may represent a restricted range of rearing experiences, which is biased toward health. More typical rearing experiences may be conducive to a higher incidence of disorders.

◆ PRELIMINARY EVALUATION

What Is the Reasoning Structure?

What are the issue and conclusion?

GENERAL ISSUE: What causes schizophrenia?
SPECIFIC ISSUE: Does schizophrenia have a genetic basis?
CONCLUSION: Schizophrenia has a genetic basis.

What are the reasons?

EMPIRICAL GENERALIZATION: More children of biologically schizophrenic mothers than of biologically non-schizophrenic mothers develop schizophrenic symptoms.

Why do the issue and conclusion matter? Getting a better sense of genetic and environmental roles in the cause of schizophrenic disorders should help us develop better ways to prevent and treat these disorders. For example, if we discover that placement in protective environments reduces the risk of schizophrenic disorders, we can work towards using environmental management techniques to help prevent and/or manage such disorders.

What terms or phrases are ambiguous?
"Genetic basis." What does this mean in terms of how genes influence schizophrenia?
"Schizophrenia." There are many schizophrenias. What was meant by schizophrenia in this study?

What perspectives underlie the reasoning? Two perspective lenses dominate in such studies: genetic and environmental causal models. Thus, it may be easy to overlook complex interactions.

◆ DETAILED LOOK AT THE STUDY

Now, let's take a closer look at Heston's study. The experimental group consisted of children removed from their schizophrenic mothers within the first three days of life and reared by nonmaternal relatives. These children were born between 1915 and 1945 to schizophrenic mothers confined to an Oregon state psychiatric hospital. Most of the children were born in the psychiatric hospital. Children were included in the study if the mother's hospital record (1) specified a diagnosis of schizophrenia, dementia praecox, or psychosis; (2) contained sufficient descriptions of a thinking disorder or bizarre regressed behavior to substantiate the diagnosis; (3) showed no evidence of syphilis or other diseases with known psychiatric manifestations; and (4) contained presumptive evidence that mother and child had been separated at birth. No attempt was made to assess the psychiatric status of the father. Of the 74 offspring born to such mothers, 27 were dropped from the study, most because of early death or contact with their maternal relatives, leaving a final sample of 47 children (30 males and 17 females). This group was followed up and interviewed in 14 states and Canada when they were at a mean age of 36.

The control group consisted of offspring born to apparently normal mothers over the same time period. For those experimental children sent to orphanages (about half of group), a like number of control subjects were selected from the same homes, matched for sex, type of eventual placement, and for length of time in child-care institutions. Those experimental children who went directly into foster or adopting families were matched with controls who had spent up to a maximum of three months in the foundling homes. Control subjects were eliminated if their mothers had any record of psychiatric hospitalization. Maternal death and desertion were the most frequent reasons for the children being in an orphanage. The 50 control children were also followed up at a mean age of 36.

Many kinds of information about the subjects were acquired. Background information included police and Veterans Administration records, credit reports, school records, civil and criminal court actions, newspaper files, public psychiatric hospital records, and others. In addition, for most subjects, a psychiatric assessment included a personal interview, a Minnesota Multiphasic Personality Inventory (MMPI), an I.Q. test score, the social class of the subject's first home, and the subject's current social class. Subjects were asked to participate in a personal interview, structured as a general medical and environmental questionnaire, which explored all important psychosocial dimensions in considerable depth. Most interviews were conducted in the homes of the subjects, and the short form of the MMPI was given after the interview. All of the investigations and interviews were conducted by the author of the study.

Heston states that the dossier compiled on each subject, excluding genetic and institutional information, was evaluated blindly and independently by two psychiatrists and that he did a third evaluation himself. The most important evaluation measure for our purposes was a psychiatric diagnosis from the American Psychiatric Association nosology. In disputed cases of psychiatric diagnoses (total number is not specified), a fourth psychiatrist was asked for an opinion and differences were discussed in conference. Complete agreement on four diagnoses—schizophrenia, mental deficiency, sociopathic personality, and neurotic personality disorder—was reported. The rate of psychiatric disability was much greater in the experimental than in the control group. *Five* of the 47 experimental group versus *none* of the 50 control children were judged as schizophrenic at follow-up. Also, other psychiatric diagnoses were much more frequent in the experimental group: for example, sociopathic personality, 9 versus 2, and neurotic personality disorder, 13 versus 7. The author states that about one-half of the experimental group showed major psychosocial disability. Heston concludes that this study supports a genetic etiology of schizophrenia.

◆ ADVANCED EVALUATION

How Good Is the Evidence?

How generalizable is the sample?   Let's first take a look at the biological parents. How representative were they of individuals with schizophrenic disorders? The original sample size of 74 was quite large. However, 15 of these children died before achieving school age, and another 12 were eliminated from the study for a variety of other reasons. These findings suggest that these biological parents as a whole may have been less physically healthy than the general population, and prenatal birth problems may have been quite high. The initial sample was not a random selection of individuals diagnosed as schizophrenic. All were confined to one state psychiatric hospital in the Northwest, and any selective factors associated with placement in this hospital restrict generalizability. Also, Heston states that selection requirements meant that the mothers as a group were biased in the direction of severe, chronic disease. The research report gives no information about length of hospitalization of the mothers, their intelligence, or their social adjustment prior to developing schizophrenia. Thus, the sample of biological mothers seems quite biased. Different results, for example, might have occurred if more mildly disturbed mothers had been sampled, especially if it is the case that there exist different kinds of schizophrenic disorders.

How about the sample of mothers of adopted children whose biological mothers were not schizophrenic? Heston strived to match control children for sex, type of eventual placement, and for length of time in child-care institutions. He gives no information on the background of their parents, but does state that he ruled out any parents who had a psychiatric hospital record. Thus, we do not know how typical these "normal" parents were. It is reasonable to suspect that mothers who give up their children at birth may differ in important ways from mothers who don't. We can also ask how generalizable the sample of foster homes, adoptive parents, and institutions was. Heston's report gives no descriptive information about these placement settings. Thus, we do not know how generalizable such placements are. For example, are these placements providing especially good care? bad care?

How valid are the measurements and the experimental manipulations? Can we count on the diagnoses of the parents and of the children? Diagnoses of these parents were made between 1915 and 1945, and the diagnosis of schizophrenic disorders has changed markedly over the years. No reliability data is given on diagnoses made at the psychiatric hospital. What does seem clear is that these mothers showed chronic severe symptoms, indicating that they were suffering from *some* serious psychiatric disorder.

The diagnosis of the children was very ambitious and included much relevant diagnostic information, and all major psychiatric diagnoses showed unanimous opinion among two psychiatrists and the author, providing strong support for the reliability of the diagnosis. However, agreement among raters does not prove validity of ratings; and the fact that the author completed all interviews himself and also prepared the diagnostic dossiers, suggests the possibility of the experimenter biasing effects in the diagnostic process affecting validity. Also, these diagnoses were made in the mid-1960s, prior to some major shifts in the definition of schizophrenia. Only a total of 5 subjects were diagnosed as schizophrenic. Heston's article, however, does not make clear the basis for these diagnoses, and it would be helpful to know how clear-cut such diagnoses were. It is possible in a study such as this that assessors, knowing the purpose of the study, may have a tendency to overdiagnose when in doubt.

This study involved no experimental manipulations.

Are there rival causes? What might account for the differences in the rates of schizophrenia between the two groups, other than genetic differences? Here are a few:

1. Selective placements. Were children of hospitalized schizophrenic parents placed into different kinds of homes than children of "normal" parents? Possibly.

2. Diagnostic biases. Although two judges made "blind" diagnoses, the information they were using was compiled by Heston, who was not blind. Could the information have been biased?

3. Differences in prenatal environments. It seems highly likely that the hospitalized schizophrenic parents may have had less healthy prenatal environments than children of nonhospitalized parents. For example, was there greater malnutrition, or a higher rate of viral infections in these mothers? Also, is there a greater chance of birth injury in a hospital setting that may predispose a child to a schizophrenic disorder?

Are any statistics deceptive?   None which are obvious. One concern is the low frequency of diagnoses of schizophrenia in the experimental group, which led to the conclusion of a significant statistical difference. That is, the magnitude of the differences between the two groups is quite small; the experimental group does not show a high rate of schizophrenia. If there was much diagnostic bias in the assessors, then we need to be careful about how strongly we weight the significance of these numbers. For example, a finding of only four diagnoses of schizophrenic disorder in the experimental group and of one schizophrenic disorder in the control group would have led to non-significant findings.

What significant information is omitted?   What was the general health status of the schizophrenic mothers? Did they have more birth complications than the normal mothers? Did the quality of the foster homes, adoptive parents, or institutions differ? How similar were the diagnostic criteria of schizophrenia in the years 1915 to 1945, and in the mid-1960s, to present definitions of schizophrenia? How reliable were the original hospital diagnoses? Did Heston and the other two psychiatrists diagnosing the foster-home-reared children use criteria for diagnosing schizophrenia that are typical of today's criteria?

How does Heston's research fit into the broader context of research on the genetics of schizophrenia, such as other family, twin, and adoption studies? Have Heston's results been replicated by others using more modern diagnostic methods, which rely heavily on specific criteria and which may be more reliable than those used years ago?

What conclusions are justified by the evidence? These data are quite consistent with the hypothesis that genetic factors can predispose individuals to schizophrenic disorders. However, the data also can be explained by several other plausible hypotheses. Thus, our conclusion must be very tentative. A reasonable, qualified conclusion is that children of severely psychiatrically disturbed parents are vulnerable to adult schizophrenia if it can be established that the diagnosis of schizophrenia in this study fits more recent conceptions of schizophrenia. Much more research is required before any strong conclusions can be drawn about the role of genetics in schizophrenia.

Turning on the Transfer Switch

Adoption studies should be very easy to spot because their primary purpose will be to study genetic factors as causes, and they will be referred to explicitly as adoption studies. They are especially pervasive in studies of the hereditability of intelligence and schizophrenia.

Transfer Study
Many investigators believe that alcoholism is due to biological causes. For example, Goodwin et al., 1973, compared a group of adoptees who had biological parents who were alcoholic with a group whose biological parents were not alcoholic. They reported that by the age of 30, those with alcoholic biological parents showed significantly higher rates of alcohol abuse than those with nonalcoholic biological parents. Since all adoptees were reared in nonalcoholic environments, the different alcoholism rates suggest that a predisposition to develop alcoholism may be inherited.

CHAPTER 13

General Issue: How Should We Treat Abnormal Behavior?

Research Approach: Outcome Studies

Topic highlighted: Psychotherapy

Are some therapies superior to others? Sloane and his colleagues (Sloane et al., 1975) compared the effects of psychoanalytic therapy and behavior therapy on college students who sought treatment at a university outpatient clinic. They randomly assigned participants to either psychoanalytic therapy, behavior therapy, or a waiting-list control condition. Both treatment groups received four months of therapy from experienced clinicians. Results immediately following treatment showed that both behavior therapy and psychoanalytic therapy produced significantly greater improvement than did the waiting-list control condition, but were not significantly different from each other. Therapeutic gains were maintained at a follow-up evaluation eight months later, with no significant differences between the two treatment approaches. This study suggests different therapies have similar effects.

Mental health treatment in the United States has become a major industry. Increasing numbers of people are seeking treatment for mental health problems, the number of persons employed in helping such people is rapidly expanding, and the amount of money spent for such treatments steadily increases. For example, by the 1970s, more than 6 million Americans were receiving some form of psychotherapy in clinics and in hospitals. From 1975 to 1990, the number of psychiatrists increased from 26,000 to 36,000, clinical psychologists from 15,000 to 42,000, clinical social workers from 25,000 to 80,000, and marriage and family counselors from 6,000 to 40,000. A recent government estimate is that the direct economic costs of mental health care is close to $55 billion per year (NIMH, 1991: 29).[1]

Are we getting our money's worth? This dramatic growth in mental health services raises many important questions, and among the most important are questions about psychotherapy, such as the following. Does psychotherapy work? Are some forms of psychotherapy more effective than others? Are specific forms of psychotherapy best for specific kinds of clients? Are some therapists more effective than others? What are the most important helping factors in psychotherapy? These are all important questions for psychotherapy researchers.

High-quality psychotherapy research is often very expensive and time-consuming. Because it is impossible to complete the perfect psychotherapy study, researchers strive to fit pieces into the massive psychotherapy effectiveness puzzle. One of the most common important research procedures is a psychotherapy *outcome study*, in which researchers vary the kinds of treatments various groups receive to determine whether some treatments work more effectively than others. Outcome studies vary greatly in complexity, but the most ambitious ones all try to randomly assign clinical cases to treatment and control groups and to rule out as many rival causes as possible to explain differences between the groups.

Outcome researchers must confront numerous tricky research problems. As critical thinkers wanting to make judgments about the effectiveness of psychotherapies, we need to be especially sensitive to two of these.

Perhaps the biggest obstacle to outcome research is finding valid measures of mental health; thus, an extremely important critical thinking question is, "How valid are the measures?" Outcome study conclusions are often worded like the following. More clients in Group A *improved* than in Group B. Treatment X has a 60 percent *cure* rate. Therapy X proved its *effectiveness*. Two-thirds of the patients *got better* when treated with X. Our natural question should be what criteria have the researchers used to determine the meaning of

[1]Kirk, Stuart A. & Kutchins, H. (1993). *The Selling of DSM*, New York: Aldine de Gruyter: pp. 8–9.

"improved," "cured," "effectiveness," or "got better." and how much can we depend on these measures?

Let's contemplate the problem. If I wanted to know whether you had "gotten better" as a result of seeing a psychotherapist, which of the following ways of finding out do you think makes the most sense? Asking you? Asking your therapist? Asking your spouse or other family members? Asking your best friend? Carefully observing your behavior for a period of time? Giving you a psychological test? Putting you under stress to see how you respond? And what if the answers disagree? You think you're in great mental health, but your therapist believes you're having a manic episode. Or, you think you need more therapy, but your friends think you're doing great. I think you can see the problem that researchers face. They must choose from a host of possible ways to measure mental health—criteria measures—all of which pose major problems for generalizing about the effects of treatments on mental health.

One way to assess mental health status is to *ask* participants to rate their present state of mental health. Such self-reports are prone to many response biases and distortions. For example, to please her therapist, a therapy participant may report feeling much better than she truly feels. In addition, the *meaning* of a self-report is highly dependent on theoretical preferences. For example, behaviorists are much more likely to accept clients' conscious reports as valid indicators or mental health status than are psychodynamically oriented therapists.

Reports by observers, such as ratings by the therapist or by acquaintances are another measurement possibility. Observer judgments, however, are not objective-free of biases and distortions. Also, how a person feels on the inside may not be well reflected by her observable behaviors. For example, elation on the outside may be hiding inner depressive feelings. Behaviorally oriented clinicians have stressed careful self-recording and/or observer recording, but such records are also subject to distortion and often oversimplify the meaning of psychological health. To illustrate the complexity of the problem, let me list a sample of the variety of outcome measures that have been used in psychotherapy research: symptom complaint checklists, self-reported and observer-reported frequencies of specific behaviors, frequencies of specific disruptive thoughts, spousal reports of employment, parental reports of childhood problems, therapists' reports or ratings of symptoms, direct observation or monitoring of specific problem behaviors, heart rate, brain wave patterns, personality tests, and self-esteem measures.

The fact that different therapies claim different goals further complicates the issue. For example, behavioral therapists may focus on goals that can be defined and measured in behavioral terms—like the number of panic attacks experienced in the last month—while psychoanalysts might be quite suspicious of behavioral and self-reported data and prefer to emphasize therapist judgment of insight as the relevant criterion. Thus, these and other complexities related to how we measure mental health alert us to the need to stress the question "How valid are the measures?" If measures tell us therapy participants are better, can we be sure that they are actually better?

A second major hurdle for outcome researchers is that they must seek satisfactory answers to the question, "What is it about taking part in a specific therapy that makes someone's mental health improve when many factors may cause improvement?" For example, one group of factors is called *non-specific factors*, which are factors common to most therapies, such as therapist warmth and empathy and ability to arouse hope in clients. Another important factor is *participant expectancy*. People often get better, not because of something specific that goes on in the therapy, but because being in therapy creates high expectations for change, and these may facilitate change. Such expectancy effects are called *placebo effects*. Because of these rival causes and others, multiple control groups are desirable as a way to rule out rival causes. Thus, an important question we must ask of this research is, "How well have the researchers used control groups to rule out rival causes?" Knowing that we must be especially sensitive to the problem of measuring change and to the problem of rival causes, let's now take a look at our opening study in more detail.

◆ PRELIMINARY EVALUATION

What Is the Structure
of the Reasoning?

What are the issue and conclusion?

GENERAL ISSUE: Which therapy is most effective?

SPECIFIC ISSUE: Which therapy is more effective: psychoanalytic or behavior therapy?

CONCLUSION: Psychoanalytic and behavioral therapies may be equally effective (empirical generalization).

What are the reasons? Research evidence: Both behavior therapy and psychoanalytic therapy produced significantly greater improvement than did the waiting-list control condition, but were not significantly different from each other. Therapeutic gains were maintained at follow-up evaluation, with no significant differences between the two treatment approaches.

Why do the issue and conclusion matter? Consumers of psychotherapy services need to make informed choices about psychotherapy and psychotherapists. Getting a clear answer to this issue should weed out ineffective therapies and provide the public with useful information for deciding whether to seek psychotherapy and what kind of therapy to seek, if they should so choose. Also, insurance and managed care organizations must make decisions on what kinds of mental health treatments they will support, and well-done outcome studies could potentially help them make such decisions.

What terms or phrases are ambiguous?
    "College students." What college? What problems were they experiencing?
    "Psychoanalytic therapy." What kind of psychoanalytic therapy? Traditional? Five times a week? Once a week?
    "Behavior therapy." What kind of behavior therapy?
    "Experienced clinicians." How experienced?
    "Greater improvement." How improved were the clients?

What perspectives underlie the reasoning? Psychoanalytic and behavioral theories do. This means that assumptions about what constitutes "getting better" will differ, and that biological factors will be pushed into the background.

◆ ADVANCED EVALUATION

Further Details of the Study

Although Sloane et al.'s study had many aims, the one most relevant to our purposes was to compare the effectiveness of behavior therapy, analytically-oriented therapy (which they referred to as "psychotherapy", and minimal contact (being on a waiting list) treatment.
    At the Temple University Psychiatric Outpatient Clinic, as

many patients as possible were screened for the study and came from a variety of sources: the health services of nearby colleges, referrals from local hospitals without adequate psychiatric facilities, self-referrals, and the local community mental health center. To select patients, one of three assessors evaluated the patient's suitability for the study, determined the main problems ("target symptoms"), rated the severity of these problems, and rated the patient's adjustment in other areas of life. The assessors reevaluated each patient after four months of treatment and again approximately one year after the initial contact. A research assistant prepared patients for their assessments, maintained telephone contact with waiting-list patients (the latter had been told that crisis help was available if needed) to reassure them that treatment would be forthcoming, and at the time of each assessment, also interviewed a close friend or relative of the patient ("informant") to obtain additional perspectives on the patient's status. Patients were also seen two years after the initial assessment by the research assistant. The three assessors varied in psychiatric training and interests. All had treated large numbers of patients (ranging from 300 to 1200). Two were primarily psychoanalytic in orientation, and one was primarily behavioral. The research assistant was a college graduate in her early twenties with no formal graduate training.

The two main measures of treatment outcome were: (1) changes in severity of three target symptoms, determined individually for each patient in the initial assessment session, and (2) changes in general adjustment (as rated by the assessor, the patient, the therapist, and the informant). Because the assessors could be regarded as the most impartial evaluators of the patient's status, their ratings were accorded greater weight than the ratings of other sources.

Researchers used four criteria to accept patients: (1) appropriateness for outpatient psychotherapy (they excluded relatively normal or situationally disturbed persons and psychotic, drug-abusing, suicidal, or brain-damaged persons); (2) willingness to participate in four months of "talking therapy"; (3) judgment by assessors that psychotherapy was the treatment of choice; (4) range in age of between 18 and 45 years old. These criteria led to the acceptance of 94 and rejection of 29 patients. Most selected patients were in their early twenties, female (60%) and white (92%), had an average of fourteen years of education, and had achieved a verbal intelligence score of 99 on a rough measure of intelligence. Fifty-four percent were students.

Most patients (71%) were born and raised in a large city, and 52% were living at home. Only 26% had been married at the time of initial assessment. Average Minnesota Multiphasic Personality Inventory (MMPI) scores were in the abnormal range (T > 70) on four scales. About two-thirds of the sample were diagnosed by assessors as carrying neurotic diagnoses. About two-thirds were given a DSM diagnosis of Anxiety Reaction. The most commonly rated patient reported target symptoms were anxiety (20%), inability to perform in some area of behavior (17%); unwanted habits (12%); and bodily complaints (11%). The average severity of initial target symptoms was 3.10, 3.17, and 3.13 for the behavior therapy, psychotherapy, and wait-list groups, using a severity rating scale that ranged from 0 = absent to 4 = severe. Almost two-thirds of the patients said they had previously participated in formal psychotherapy, and 7 percent of patients with previous psychiatric contact had received medication.

The researchers matched patients on number per group (30), level of neuroticism (based on scores on a personality test), and gender. Also, high, medium, and low therapist-experience levels were represented in each treatment group. Behavior therapy and psychotherapy patients were given four months of weekly, hour-long therapy (an average of 13.2 and 14.2 sessions, respectively), and control patients spent four months on the wait list. Therapists were free to use whatever techniques they thought appropriate for particular patients.

The researchers found that the severity of target symptoms had decreased significantly in both the behavior therapy and psychotherapy groups, relative to changes in the minimal treatment group, and that the two treated groups did not differ from one another. For both active treatments the average severity of symptoms decreased from moderately severe to trivial-to-mild, whereas the average severity of symptoms in the minimal treatment group remained within the mild-to-moderate range. However, the groups did not differ in average general adjustment as assessed by structured interview assessment.

In terms of target symptom severity, 80% of the patients in the behavioral and analytically oriented treatment groups were rated by assessors as improved or recovered compared with only 48% of the patients in the minimal treatment group. With respect to assessors' rating of overall adjustment, the percentages of patients rated as improved or recovered in the behavioral, analytically oriented, and minimal-treatment groups were 93%, 77%, and 77%, respectively. Self-ratings of improved or recovered characterized 74%, 81%, and 44% of the patients in the behavioral, psychotherapy, and minimal-treatment groups, respectively. On self-ratings of overall adjustment, the respective percentages for the behavioral, psychotherapy, and minimal-treatment patients were 93%, 80%, and 55%.

Sloane et al. obtained follow-up data on all but two of the original participants who once again met with and were evaluated by their assessors. Change evident at four months had continued in a favorable direction or had been maintained. Sloane et al. concluded: "It is remarkable that all three groups of patients significantly improved in four months. The control group was by no means 'untreated,' but it improved considerably without any formal therapy. Nevertheless, both groups of formally treated patients improved significantly more than the control patients on their target symptoms. This is rather clear evidence that therapy in general 'works'" (pp. 223–224).

◆ ADVANCED EVALUATION

How Good Is the Evidence?

This study is among the most ambitious outcome studies that has ever been conducted, one that has many strengths and has been widely praised. As well-done as it was, however, we will discover in our evaluation a number of problems that clearly illustrate the difficulty of conducting an informative outcome study.

How generalizable is the sample?   The patient sample size of 30 per treatment is quite large for such a study. In terms of breadth, however, we can only generalize to "neurotic" patients who are not extremely disturbed, who are judged appropriate for treatment at clinics such as this one, and who are primarily white, unmarried, attending college, ranging in age from 18 to 45, and willing to take part in a research study. A major limitation to generalization is that the patient sample is not random and is subject to major sampling biases. One bias is that awareness by referral sources of an ongoing research project markedly affects the referral process. For example, if referral sources want to be sure to have patients get behavior therapy, they will be reluctant to refer them to the clinic if they are aware of the research project. In fact, often in studies like these, the number of referrals drop off markedly when the study is publicized, because of referral source concerns about referring patients to ongoing research projects. Indeed, Sloane et al. report such a problem in their study.

How valid are the measures and the experimental manipulations? A strength of this study is the use of multiple sources—assessor, therapist, and patient—to assess outcome. However, each source is subject to many biases, especially expectancy biases. Sloane et al. relied most heavily on assessor ratings, and these would seem to be most free of bias, especially if the assessors were blind to the treatment group in which a patient had participated. However, it is likely that patients would provide cues hinting at the nature of their treatment, or in the case of the waiting-list control group, the lack of treatment, and that these cues could bias the assessment. Therapist and patient alike have strong motivation to make the therapy appear successful, thus biasing these ratings. An interesting finding of this study is that assessor ratings and patient ratings correlated quite highly (although exhibiting many marked discrepancies), while assessor and therapist ratings showed no relationship! Many reviewers of this study have commented on the high improvement rate shown by the minimal treatment group; it seems too good to be true. After four months, 77% of these patients were rated as improved in overall adjustment by the assessors (the same percentage as in the psychotherapy group even if lower than the 93% in the behavior therapy group). One possibility is that assessors were quite lenient in their judgments.

Sloane et al. provide no reliability and validity data concerning the measures they used to assess improvement; we need such measures to help us decide just how valid these criteria might be.

Did these patients *truly* improve? That is an unanswerable question because our willingness to accept any index of improvement depends on someone's definition of the term "improvement." If a client says she has improved, and her therapist says she has not, has she truly improved? Our answer must be, "It depends on what meaning of 'improvement' on which we are willing to agree." Thus, in this study, as in all psychotherapy outcome studies, each of us as readers must decide for ourselves how well the outcome measures used generalize to our own concepts of mental health. This study should clearly remind us that we can never *truly know* someone's mental health, and that there are no *pure* measures of mental health.

We need to ask two important questions about the generalizability of the therapy treatments, those concerning the experimental manipulations in the study. First, are the *skills* of these therapists typical of therapists in general? Second, have the therapists within each theoretical orientation conducted therapy in the way therapy is typically conducted? We have a small, select group of therapists for each treatment, greatly limiting generalizability. All were white males. All but one was a psychiatrist. The authors report that all were considered good therapists by their peers, and enjoyed excellent professional reputations. Although experience varied markedly, all six therapists had treated at least 250 patients and had at least six years of practice experience. They also were secure enough about their skills to participate in this study. Thus, we can only generalize to a population of similarly trained therapists.

Therapists were free to use whatever therapeutic techniques they felt to be most appropriate for each individual patient, and therapy was time-limited—less than four months. Thus, we can only generalize to populations of therapists who practice in a manner similar to the way these six therapists applied their therapy orientation in time-limited therapy. If the usual length of therapy practiced outside the research setting for these kinds of problems is shorter or longer than that permitted in this study, then generalization from this study is severely limited. We should wonder how representative of psychoanalytic and behavioral therapies in general were the applications of therapy in this study. For example, if these therapists were especially conscientious in applying their techniques because they knew that they were involved in an important research study and that their results would be scrutinized, then generalization would be limited. In all therapy outcome studies, we need to ask, "How representative of therapy practice in general is the practice taking place in the research study?"

What are the rival causes?   Did these patients show improvement on measures of outcome because of their therapy? One possible rival cause explaining the differences between active treatment groups and the control group is the *attention* received from the therapists. Both treatment groups received an average of fourteen hours of attention from their therapists, while the waiting-list control subjects received no such attention. Another possible rival cause is *patient ex-*

pectancy of getting better because of a treatment. Perhaps patients got better because they thought treatment should make them better. Patients in the waiting-list control group, who improved in surprisingly large numbers, possibly due to strong expectancy effects, still could not be expected to have their hopes raised as much as those who thought they were receiving a helpful treatment. In addition, control subjects would be expected to feel less of a demand to please the assessors. Also, the lack of differences between treatment groups could have been caused by therapists in one group being superior in ability to those in the other group. Such differences could have overridden differences in specific features of the therapies that might be helpful to clients.

Are there any deceptive statistics? These researchers are very thorough in presenting their results, providing both statistics on mean differences among the groups and detailed tables showing the percentages of people who changed in each group. An important question to ask in all psychotherapy outcome research is, "How *clinically meaningful* are the changes?" The answer to that question depends on the meaningfulness of an "improved" rating. For example, very few clients in any of the groups were rated as "recovered." We have to be careful not to interpret the data to mean that high percentages of patients recovered from their problems.

What significant information is omitted? Were assessors truly blind to group membership of patients? How similar was the administration of the treatments in the study to the way such treatments are typically administered? Why did all three groups show such a high improvement rate? Would different kinds of patients have responded differently? What results would a two-year followup provide? How does this study fit into the overall context of outcome-study research? Do any more recent studies show significant differences between treatments?

What conclusions are justified by the evidence? Our conclusion must be highly qualified, and we must avoid overgeneralizing. We can conclude that when individuals with rather select problems are referred in some biased fashion to a treatment study and then exposed to intense involvement in a therapy research experience, most will provide evidence that the treatments have helped them, regardless of the kind of therapy they receive. We can't know how people in general, or people with quite different problems, would respond to therapists' practicing as they typically do in the real world, when they know they are not involved in a research study. We would certainly want to view this study as only one in a large matrix of potential psychotherapy studies, hoping to eventually form a coherent picture of the relationships among kinds of therapies, qualities of therapists, and qualities of clients.

Turning on the Transfer Switch

> Xanax seen as effective treatment for panic disorders!
> Cognitive therapy: treatment of choice for depression!

Such claims should alert us. We should see them whenever someone is promoting a particular therapy, whether a talking therapy or a drug therapy. Outcome studies of drug treatments are especially ubiquitous in today's society, and appear often in major adds for drugs. Certainly, if your doctor is prescribing drugs for a family relative, you might ask him for outcome study evidence.

Whenever we encounter claims of a therapy's effectiveness, we first should try to turn on the critical-question switch: "How do they know it's effective?" And then, we should be alert to the possibility of the authors' using outcome studies to support their claims. We should be on the lookout for such key phrases as "successful treatment," "better results," and "performing better than the control group." Once we can say, "That's an outcome study," we should turn on our critical-thinking switch for outcome studies.

Transfer Study
Some forms of therapy are as effective as drugs in treating depression. In a recent investigation of 250 patients who were either moderately or severely depressed, patients were divided at random into three experimental groups: The first and second groups were treated with one of two types of brief psychotherapy, designed to last sixteen weeks, while the third group was given the drug imipramine. A control group of patients received placebos in addition to weekly supportive consultations with a psychiatrist. A total of 50 to 60 percent of patients who received either the psychotherapeutic treatments or the drug reached "full recovery" with no serious symptoms, but fewer than 30 percent of those in the control group reached full recovery.

References

ALLOY, L.B. & ABRAMSON, L.Y. (1979). Judgment of contingency in depressed and nondepressed students: Sadder but wiser? *Journal of Experimental psychology: General, 108,* 441–485.

BREIER, A., CHARNEY, D.S., & HENINGER, G.R. (1986). Agoraphobia with panic attacks: Development, diagnostic stability, and course of illness. *Archives of General Psychiatry, 43,* 1029–1036.

BROWN, G.W. & HARRIS, T. (1978). *Social origins of depression.* London: Tavistock.

BUCHSBAUM, M.S. & HAIER, R.J. (1987). Functional and anatomical brain imaging: Impact on schizophrenia research. *Schizophrenia Bulletin, 13,* 115–132.

BUCHSBAUM, M.S., INGVAR, D.H., KESSLER, R., WATERS, R.N., CAPPELLETTI, J., VAN KAMMEN, D.P., KING, A.C., JOHNSON, J.L., MANNING, R.G., FLYNN R.W., MANN, L.S., BUNNEY, W.E., & SOKOLOFF, L. (1982). Cerebral glucography with positron tomography, *Archives of General Psychiatry, 39,* 251–259.

GOODWIN, D.W.W., SCHULSINGER, F., HERMANSEN, L., GUZE, S.B., & WINOKUS, G. (1973). Alcohol problems in adoptees raised apart from alcoholic biological parents. *Archives of General Psychiatry, 28,* 238–43.

GOTTESMAN, I.I., & SHIELDS, J. (1972). *Schizophrenia and genetics: A twin study vantage point.* New York: Academic Press.

HARRIS, E.L., NOYES, R., CROWE, R.R., & CHAUDRY, D.R. (1983). Family study of agoraphobia. *Archives of General Psychiatry, 40,* 1061–1064.

139

HESTON, L.L. (1966). Psychiatric disorders in foster home reared children of schizophrenic mothers. *British Journal of Psychiatry, 112,* 819–825.

MANOS, N., VASILOPOULOU, E., & SOTIRIOU, M. (1987). DSM-III diagnoses of borderline disorder and depression. *Journal of Personality Disorders, 1,* 263–268.

MCKEON, P., & MURRAY, R. (1987). Familial aspects of obsessive-compulsive neurosis. *British Journal of Psychiatry, 151,* 528–534.

MINEKA, S., DAVIDSON, M., COOK, M., & KEIR, R. (1984). Observational conditioning of snake fear in rhesus monkeys. *Journal of Abnormal Psychology, 93,* 355–372.

NOYES, R., CROWE, R., HARRIS, E.L., HAMRA, B.J., MCCHESNEY, C.M., & CHAUDRY, D.R. (1986). Relationship between panic disorder and agoraphobia: A family study. *Archives of General Psychiatry, 43,* 227–232.

OGATA, S.N., SILK, K.R., GOODRICH, S., et al. (1990). Childhood sexual and physical abuse in adult patients with borderline personality disorder. *American Journal of Psychiatry, 147,* 1008–1013.

ROBINS, L.N., HELZER, J.E., WEISSMAN, M.M., ORVASCHEL, H., GRUENBERG, E., BURKE, J.D., & REGIER, D.A. (1984). Lifetime prevalence of specific psychiatric disorders in three sites. *Archives of General Psychiatry, 41,* 949–958.

ROSENMAN, R.H., BRAND, R.J., JENKINS, C.D., FRIEDMAN, M., STRAUS, R., & WURM, M. (1975). Coronary heart disease in the Western Collaborative Group Study: Final follow-up experience of 8 1/2 years. *Journal of the American Medical Association, 233,* 872–877.

SHEKELLE, R.B., HULLEY, S.B., & NEATON, J.D., et al. (1985). The MRFIT behavior study. Type A behavior and incidence of coronary heart disease. *American Journal of Epidemiology, 122,* 559–70.

SLOANE, R.B., STAPLES, F.R., CRISTOL, A.H., YORKSTON, N.J., & WHIPPLE, I. (1975). *Psychoanalysis versus behavior therapy.* Cambridge: Harvard University Press.

SPITZER, R.L., FORMAN, J. & NEE, J. (1979). DSM-III field trials: I. Initial interrater diagnostic reliability. *American Journal of Psychiatry, 136,* 815–817.

SPITZER, R.L., & FORMAN, J. (1979). DSM-III field trials: II. Initial experience with the multiaxial system. *American Journal of Psychiatry, 136,* 815–817.

SWARTZ, M., BLAZER, D., GEORGE, L., & WINFIELD, I. (1990). Estimating the prevalence of borderline personality in the community. *Journal of Personality Disorders, 4,* 257–272.